Past Masters
General Editor Keith Thomas

Cervantes

Past Masters

AQUINAS Anthony Kenny
ARISTOTLE Jonathan Barnes
BACH Denis Arnold
FRANCIS BACON Anthony Quinton
BAYLE Elisabeth Labrousse
BERGSON Leszek Kolakowski
BERKELEY J. O. Urmson
THE BUDDHA Michael Carrithers
BURKE C. B. Macpherson
CARLYLE A. L. Le Quesne
CERVANTES P. E. Russell
CHAUCER George Kane
CLAUSEWITZ Michael Howard
COBBETT Raymond Williams
COLERIDGE Richard Holmes
CONFUCIUS Raymond Dawson
DANTE George Holmes
DARWIN Jonathan Howard
DIDEROT Peter France
GEORGE ELIOT Rosemary Ashton
ENGELS Terrell Carver
GALILEO Stillman Drake
GIBBON J. W. Burrow
GOETHE T. J. Reed
HEGEL Peter Singer

HOMER Jasper Griffin
HUME A. J. Ayer
JESUS Humphrey Carpenter
KANT Roger Scruton
LAMARCK L. J. Jordanova
LEIBNIZ G. MacDonald Ross
LOCKE John Dunn
MACHIAVELLI Quentin Skinner
MARX Peter Singer
MENDEL Vitezslav Orel
MILL William Thomas
MONTAIGNE Peter Burke
THOMAS MORE Anthony Kenny
WILLIAM MORRIS Peter Stansky
MUHAMMAD Michael Cook
NEWMAN Owen Chadwick
PASCAL Alban Krailsheimer
PETRARCH Nicholas Mann
PLATO R. M. Hare
PROUST Derwent May
RUSKIN George P. Landow
ADAM SMITH D. D. Raphael
TOLSTOY Henry Gifford
VICO Peter Burke
WYCLIF Anthony Kenny

Forthcoming

AUGUSTINE Henry Chadwick
BAGEHOT Colin Matthew
BENTHAM John Dinwiddy
JOSEPH BUTLER R. G. Frey
COPERNICUS Owen Gingerich
DESCARTES Tom Sorell
DISRAELI John Vincent
ERASMUS John McConica
GODWIN Alan Ryan
HERZEN Aileen Kelly
JEFFERSON Jack P. Greene
JOHNSON Pat Rogers
KIERKEGAARD Patrick Gardiner
LEONARDO E. H. Gombrich
LINNAEUS W. T. Stearn

MALTHUS Donald Winch
MONTESQUIEU Judith Shklar
NEWTON P. M. Rattansi
ROUSSEAU Robert Wokler
RUSSELL John G. Slater
SHAKESPEARE Germaine Greer
SOCRATES Bernard Williams
SPINOZA Roger Scruton
TOCQUEVILLE Larry Siedentop
VIRGIL Jasper Griffin
MARY WOLLSTONECRAFT
 William St Clair

and others

P. E. Russell

Cervantes

Withdrawn

Oxford   New York

OXFORD UNIVERSITY PRESS

1985

Oxford University Press, Walton Street, Oxford OX2 6DP

Oxford New York Toronto
Delhi Bombay Calcutta Madras Karachi
Kuala Lumpur Singapore Hong Kong Tokyo
Nairobi Dar es Salaam Cape Town
Melbourne Auckland

and associated companies in
Beirut Berlin Ibadan Nicosia

Oxford is a trade mark of Oxford University Press

First published 1985 as an Oxford University Press paperback
and simultaneously in a hardback edition

British Library Cataloguing in Publication Data

Russell, P. E.
Cervantes.—(Past Masters)
1. Cervantes Saavedra—Miguel de. Don Quixote
I. Title   II. Series
863′.3   PQ6352
ISBN 0–19–287570–1
ISBN 0–19–287569–8 pbk.

Library of Congress Cataloging in Publication Data

Russell, P. E. (Peter Edward), 1913–
Cervantes. (Past masters)
Bibliography: p.   Includes index.
1. Cervantes Saavedra, Miguel de, 1547–1616.
Don Quixote. I. Title.   II. Series.
PQ6352.R87 1985   863′.3   85–10673
ISBN 0–19–287570–1
ISBN 0–19–287569–8 (pbk.)

Set by Grove Graphics
Printed and bound in Great Britain by
Cox & Wyman Ltd, Reading

Acknowledgement

I owe special thanks to my colleague Dr J. N. H. Lawrance for his generous help with the task of revising the manuscript of this work.

Contents

Author's note   *viii*

Introduction   *1*

1   A disappointed warrior: introducing Cervantes   *5*

2   Poet and dramatist: the roads to La Mancha   *13*

3   The parodying of chivalric romance   *24*

4   What happens in *Don Quixote*: Part I   *38*

5   What happens in *Don Quixote*: Part II   *55*

6   The madness of Don Quixote   *73*

7   Art entwined with laughter   *82*

8   Don Quixote as Romantic hero   *94*

9   Conclusion   *103*

Further reading   *110*

Index   *115*

Author's note

References to *Don Quixote* in the text are given by part and chapter number. Thus 'II.16' refers to *Don Quixote* Part II, chapter 16. I have, while looking at what other translators have had to say, preferred to provide my own versions of Cervantes's texts.

Introduction

It is a truism, of course, that he [Cervantes] set the example for all other novelists to follow. (Harry Levin, *Contexts of Criticism*, 1957)

Harry Levin's comment, made here with reference to Cervantes's *Don Quixote*, echoes what many critics and many novelists themselves have said about the book for at least three centuries. Sometimes, to avoid any suggestion that *Don Quixote*'s interest for the reader nowadays is mainly a historical one, the proposition is extended into a claim that the book is 'the first modern novel'. The present study, intended particularly for English-speaking readers with no special interest in Spanish literature generally, seeks to give some account of Cervantes that will help its readers to understand why his most famous book has been singled out in this way. I have elected to discuss *Don Quixote* mainly as a masterpiece of comic writing because I think that this is the most important thing about it and the only way in which the book can be fully understood. It is, however, only fair to warn readers that, since the age of Romanticism, *Quixote* criticism has often sought to play down the comic aspects of the book, for the reasons which will be set out in Chapter 8.

Ever since the seventeenth century Cervantes's name, for most of his non-Spanish and Spanish readers alike, has, then, been associated mainly with his authorship of *Don Quixote*. But he was by no means a one-book man. He wrote a considerable number of short stories. He was the author of two long prose romances, and many plays. All his life he wrote poetry, serious and satirical. Many of these writings display his versatility as a literary craftsman as well as that unusually inventive imagination on whose possession he rightly prided himself. But only a handful of his short stories contrive, as *Don Quixote* does, to escape from what most readers will regard nowadays as too close a bondage to the literary tastes of another age. Only in *Don Quixote*, too, did Cervantes bring into existence, in the persons of the pseudo-knight and his squire, figures which possess that secret extra dimension that, from the moment of the book's first publication in 1605, enabled them to step outside the contextual limits of the work itself and to function independently of it in the enigmatic world of myth. It has therefore seemed appropriate that the present study should be mostly directed towards *Don Quixote*. Attention to Cervantes's other works will be largely restricted to features in them that can help us to interpret his most famous book.

Don Quixote, particularly Part I, was, as its printing history shows, very popular indeed with Spanish readers from the moment of its appearance. But the work was not esteemed by the Spanish literary establishment of Cervantes's day. It was, however, greatly admired in France and England, so that, for nearly two centuries after Cervantes's death in 1616, the only real critical discussion of the book came from French and English writers and critics. At the end of the eighteenth century German writers joined in the discussion with enthusiasm, though from a quite new angle. A sustained Spanish tradition of *Quixote* criticism does not really get going until the mid-nineteenth century.

By its French and English readers the book was recognized as a masterpiece and discussed as such almost from the year of its début in Spain. Thomas Shelton published the first English translation of Part I in 1612 (he had, he says, completed it several years earlier). He followed this up in 1620 with his version of Part II (five years after this had been published in Spain). César Oudin's translation of Part I into French, dedicated to Louis XIII, did not appear until 1614 but there is ample evidence that the work was already much talked about in France before then. François de Rosset's version of Part II appeared in 1618.

The printing history of *Don Quixote* illustrates dramatically the way in which the book's prestige outside Spain exceeded that which it enjoyed in Cervantes's own country. The first *de luxe* edition of *Don Quixote* ever to be published in Spanish was printed in London in 1738. The first annotated critical edition of Cervantes's text, also in Spanish, was the work of an English clergyman, John Bowle. It was published in Salisbury in 1781. English and French readers rapidly assimilated Cervantes's book into their own literary traditions and, for the most part, showed scant interest in its Spanish origins. It was only when Spaniards, late in the eighteenth century, realized the extraordinary esteem in which *Don Quixote* was held abroad that they started to confer on it the respect it deserved. If we want to understand how seventeenth- and eighteenth-century readers interpreted the book we have therefore to turn to French and English commentators.

There are strong reasons for admitting some account of Cervantes's biography to our study. One is Cervantes's own unwillingness to accept the anonymity of authorship; by the use of a variety of devices he keeps on, in *Don Quixote*, forcing his readers to think about the presence of an author, reminding them that, behind the book they are reading, there is a living personality (in several fictional disguises as well as in his own clothes) who is entitled to their attention. He has also a compulsion to introduce here as in all his other writings, reminiscences, partly fictionalized, of events taken from his personal experiences. His choice of such reminiscences, with their emphasis on military heroics, is plainly highly selective; if not balanced by a look at the other personal experiences he fails to dignify in this way, we may be misled about the relation between life and fiction in his work.

Though *Don Quixote* has been categorized as the first

modern novel, it is inextricably entwined, as a parody of the chivalry books, in the traditions of prose romance. Since a sense of the distinction between romance and novel is therefore essential to any discussion of Cervantes's book I wish to make it clear at the outset what I understand that distinction to be. I accept for working purposes the definitions set out in 1785 by an English novelist, Clara Reeve. She wrote:

> The Romance is an heroic fable which treats of fabulous persons and things. The Novel is a picture of real life and manners and of the times in which it is written. The Romance, in lofty and elevated language, describes what never happened or is likely to happen. The Novel gives a familiar relation of such things as pass every day before our eyes, such as may happen to our friend, or to ourselves; and the perfection of it is to represent every scene in so easy and natural a manner, and to make them appear so probable, as to deceive us into a persuasion (at least while we are reading) that all is real . . .

Don Quixote is a very long book. Part I contains fifty-two chapters. Part II (published in 1615) has seventy-four. Cervantes wrote when readers liked and expected the books they bought for entertainment to be lengthy. Nor is the work tightly constructed along a narrative line. Its development is arbitrary and leisurely. I have therefore thought it appropriate to devote two entire chapters to explaining something about what happens in it.

1 A disappointed warrior: introducing Cervantes

> The painful warrior famoused for fight,
> After a thousand victories once foil'd
> Is from the book of honour razed quite,
> And all the rest forgot for which he toil'd.
> (William Shakespeare, *Sonnet* 25)

Cervantes's chosen profession was that of a soldier. When his soldiering days ended he wanted to become a government official in America. His applications for an appointment there were turned down by the king, Philip II, and he had to content himself with becoming a royal tax-collector in southern Spain. He did not publish his first book until 1585, when he was getting on for forty. Twenty years then passed before the next one appeared— Part I of *Don Quixote* (1605). We know that, during these years when he described himself as sleeping 'in the silence of those who are forgotten', he was the author of many plays, most of which have disappeared. He also went on doggedly writing poems, as he had done from an early date, despite his failure to convince anyone, including himself, that he had much poetic talent. Towards the end of the twenty years he wrote, too, some of the short stories that would eventually appear in the collection he called *Exemplary Novels* (*Novelas ejemplares*), published in 1613. But it was only after the success of Part I of *Don Quixote*, when he was going on for sixty, that he was able to devote himself to full-time writing and publishing. In addition to the *Exemplary Novels* he then published the long allegorical and satirical poem about poets and poetry which he called *A Voyage to Parnassus* (*Viaje del Parnaso*, 1614). In 1615, the year of publication of Part II of *Don Quixote*, he also published a

5

selection of his plays and of the one-act 'interludes'—slight comic pieces that were performed in those days in Spain between the acts of the principal work being staged and which, nowadays, seem the only portion of Cervantes's work as a dramatist in which he mastered the art of dramatic writing (*Eight Comedies and Eight Interludes—Ocho comedias y ocho entremeses*). While he was completing *Don Quixote* Part II, he had also been writing concurrently another mammoth prose narrative very different in intention, form, and style from that book. This was a labyrinthine romantic tale of love and travel, modelled on the late Greek prose epic tradition of the early Christian era, which he called *The Labours of Persiles and Sigismunda* (*Los trabajos de Persiles y Sigismunda*). It appeared posthumously in 1617, the year after his death at the age of sixty-nine. Though Cervantes was proud of the late success with readers which *Don Quixote* had brought him, his works, up to the time of his death, continued to contain fond reminiscences of his life as an ordinary soldier in the service of the Spanish crown. Young men on their way to the wars are among the most favoured minor characters in his works. Though he was by no means silent about the less agreeable side of war, he looked back always on his days abroad as a soldier in the service of imperial Spain as the proudest ones of his life.

Miguel de Cervantes (the 'Saavedra' was a later accretion) was born in the university town of Alcalá de Henares, near Madrid, on 29 September 1547. His father was what was known as a *cirujano* or 'surgeon'. The main task of such a medical man then was to cure wounds and minor ailments and to set broken bones. The frequency with which Cervantes's father moved his family from one town to another has been held to show he was professionally unsuccessful. It may have been through contact with some of his father's patients that Miguel first developed that interest in the manifestations of insanity which he reveals in *Don Quixote* and elsewhere. The family belonged to the *hidalgo* class, that is, to the petty nobility. But in sixteenth-century Spain *hidalgos* were two-a-penny and many of them were impoverished and distinguishable from their plebeian neighbours only by their much-resented freedom from most taxation and by some other privileges. Cervantes's immediate family was, in fact, socially and economically on the way down and Cervantes himself frequently referred to the miseries of poverty. It is very noticeable that his personal experience of domestic life seems to have nothing in common with the family scenes which play a considerable part in, for example, the plots of his short stories. In these he often likes to describe well-to-do noble or bourgeois households where money is no object and a high moral tone is maintained, at least in outward appearance. In his love stories all the marriageable daughters seem to be of exceptional beauty, if sometimes of shaky virtue, and the young men, though liable to be led into sexual misbehaviour by their hot blood and machismo, are always handsome and usually ready, at least when pressure is applied, to right any wrongs they have committed. The contrived happy ending is an abiding feature of most of Cervantes's love stories and this was surely a case where he used his art to bring about imaginatively what did not come his way in life.

The important problem of Cervantes's education is very obscure. On the basis of a passage praising the Jesuit Order, specially as teachers of children at their school in Seville, it has sometimes been deduced that Cervantes was a pupil there during one of his family's stays in Andalusia. The passage occurs in one of his best and most original *novelas*, *The Colloquy of the Dogs* (*El coloquio de los perros*). However, his praise of the Jesuits is there so over-fulsome that one must suspect an inveterate ironist like Cervantes of indulging in tongue-in-cheek satire at the Jesuits' expense; in Part II of *Don Quixote* he paints an unfavourable portrait of the kind of chaplain-confessor, usually by then a Jesuit, who was liable to be found exercising what many considered excessive authority in aristocratic palaces.

Much has also been made of Cervantes's supposed attendance, about 1569, at the grammar school in Madrid run by the municipality. Its headmaster was a man who had been sympathetic in his youth to some of the ideas of the Dutch humanist Desiderius Erasmus (d. 1536), whose views on religion had caused an uproar in Spain in the opening decades of the century, though they were now forbidden reading in Philip II's kingdoms. However, chronology makes it pretty unlikely that our Cervantes can have been the 'Miguel de Cervantes' described by the headmaster of this school in 1569 as his 'cherished and dear pupil'. Even if he was, it seems improbable that any headmaster appointed by the Madrid municipality in the conformist 1560s would have dared to pass on any unorthodox Erasmist views to his pupils. Nevertheless the fact remains that somewhere during his boyhood Cervantes acquired an excellent secondary education and a love of reading.

One thing appears certain: Cervantes did not go to a university, though he seems to have wished that he had. Students and graduates very often appear as major or minor characters in his books. He usually makes his students cheerful, relaxed, and witty figures. The University of Salamanca is mentioned so frequently that it has sometimes been concluded he must himself have been a student there. But a careful examination of these passages fails to reveal any inside knowledge or experience of university life and, more tellingly, his writings make it plain that Cervantes had no respect for the style of thinking and writing, highly dependent on authority, precedent, and tradition, which ruled the Spanish universities in his time. All the same he may have felt some unease among his peers because of his lack of a university education. At times, for example, he seems to go out of his way to show that he is familiar with the accepted authorities on a given intellectual topic such as the then fashionable neo-Aristotelian theories about the nature of literature or the metaphysical basis of Platonic ideas about love.

One established aspect of Cervantes's literary education needs to be mentioned here. When he was a boy he says that he saw the stage performances of a famous actor-manager of that time, Lope de Rueda (d. 1565), who was also a playwright. This left him with a lifelong love of the drama and the world of the theatre and a desire to become a dramatist himself. It was to prove an unfortunate obsession in later years. The comments on actors and acting scattered through his own dramatic and non-dramatic writings suggest that one of the things that attracted him to the theatre was his abiding interest in the illusory reality which it was the business of dramatist and actors between them to create.

In 1569 Cervantes suddenly left Spain for Italy. He would not return for eleven years. By 1570, he had enlisted as a soldier in one of the crack Spanish infantry regiments stationed in Naples, then the centre of Spanish rule in Italy. The next five years he spent on active service in various parts of the Mediterranean. Cervantes took part in the famous naval victory over the Turkish fleet off Lepanto, in the Gulf of Corinth, in November 1571. He was wounded in the action and permanently lost the use of his left hand. Independent contemporary evidence confirms that he behaved with outstanding bravery in the battle. Right up to the end of his life he never tired of referring to Lepanto and his part in that 'prodigious feat of arms', as he called it.

Cervantes has nothing of much interest to say about Italy in his writings. However he does seem to have taken the trouble to learn enough Italian to read books in it, among them those of the great Italian masters of the short story (*novella*)—Boccaccio, Bandello, Giraldi Cinthio and others—and learnt from them how to become, as he said many years later, the first Spanish author to cultivate this form of writing. Cervantes was at this time still an avid and impressionable reader of the many prose romances of chivalry that Spanish authors had shown themselves to be adept at fabricating. Now, in Italy, he also read the burlesque epic poems on traditional chivalric themes composed by Italian poets of the early Renaissance like Luigi Pulci, Matteo Maria Boiardo, and, most delicately ironic of them all, Ludovico Ariosto. In Ariosto's *Orlando Furioso* (*The Madness of Roland*) the spirit of chivalry is burlesqued and made the target for the poet's wit while nevertheless still granted imaginative authenticity and a measure of sympathy and respect for what drives its heroes and heroines and even its villains. When, thirty years later, Cervantes came in *Don Quixote* to write his burlesque of the Spanish chivalric romances he had once read and loved, he not only showed that he remembered Ariosto's narrative technique; his admiration for Ariosto's poem seems to have pulled him away from the unsympathetic parody of chivalric romance which he evidently had in mind when he started out to write the story that eventually became the book that would make him famous.

In 1575, his term of service in Italy completed, Miguel sailed for Spain. He was unfit for further employment as a soldier but he carried with him letters of special recommendation to the king from Don John of Austria and other notables so that the chances of a good job must have looked promising. But soldierly pride soon turned to humiliation when the galley on which he was travelling was attacked and captured by a Turkish squadron working out of Algiers, and he found himself a prisoner of the hated infidel. In accordance with a custom long practised by both Spaniards and Turks, Miguel was sold into slavery in Algiers, joining the many other Spanish prisoners held in like state there. They could only hope for release if their families raised the ransom money demanded by their owners. The letters Miguel carried made his captors think he was more important than he was so that the sum required for his release was correspondingly high.

Cervantes now spent five years as a prisoner in Algiers. Memories of the experience abound in his works. In his literary treatment of his captivity there is a good deal of ambiguity. On the one hand he entirely accepts and fuels the claims of contemporary Spanish anti-Turkish and anti-Muslim propaganda, stressing the inhumanity of the Turks. But there are also unexplained inconsistencies in his allusions to his captivity. Documentary evidence shows that he was an active organizer of escape attempts, the penalty for which was death. Yet his master, Hassan Pasha, the governor of Algiers, whom he denounces by name for his cruelty, treated him on these occasions with quite extraordinary leniency. Moreover the Spanish captives by Cervantes's own account in fact enjoyed a considerable degree of freedom and religious tolerance. This, too, is sometimes reflected in his literary descriptions of their life and of the Algerian scene in general, both of which he recorded in his memory with a writer's eye for the exotic and for the other manifestations of a strange culture. We see this at work, for instance, in *Don Quixote* in the story of 'The Captive Captain' ('El capitán cautivo') which depicts a romantic attachment between a Christian prisoner and a Moorish lady (I.39–41). Cervantes, one way and another, got a good deal of mileage out of his captivity in Algiers. It is quite possible that, paradoxically, it represented one of the most fulfilled periods of his life. His escape attempts and his general refusal to be intimidated by his captors made him a well-known personality among the prisoners and seems to have earned him the unwilling respect of the Turks too. Miguel's ransom of 500 escudos was finally paid by his family in 1580, apparently just before Hassan Pasha, whose term of office in Algiers was over, was due to sail for Constantinople taking Cervantes with him. Had that happened it is unlikely that anything more would have been heard of the future author of *Don Quixote*.

If Cervantes expected to get a deferred hero's welcome in Spain he was speedily undeceived. Captivity had been the foil that had caused his warrior's deeds to be forgotten there. Soon we find him on the look-out for a post in America, then a sure sign of desperation. Meanwhile he had decided to seek to break into the world of literature by trying his hand at the most fashionable narrative fictional form of the time, and one which Spaniards had given to late sixteenth-century Europe—the pastoral romance. The result was *La Galatea* (1585).

Cervantes's career as a soldier thus brought him no material rewards and left him physically mutilated and socially marginalized. But the years of disappointment and humiliation that lay immediately ahead never seem to have succeeded in shaking his defiant pride in his soldierly past or his determination to defend traditional military and patriotic values. The fact that his irrepressible instinct for irony eventually caused him to make Don Quixote also one of their defenders in no way justifies the conclusion that, by 1605, he had become disillusioned with such values. The worthwhileness of heroism would be the theme of his Christian quest romance, *Persiles and Sigismunda*.

2 Poet and dramatist: the roads to La Mancha

'I liken poetry, sir, to a young, tender virgin of surpassing beauty, whom many other virgins, that is to say all the other sciences, have the duty of embellishing, ornamenting and informing.' (*Don Quixote* II.16)

Believing that the world was still the same as when my praises were abroad, I again composed some plays. But I found no birds in yesteryear's nests. I mean I found no managers who wanted them, though they knew I had them. (Cervantes in the prologue to *Eight Comedies and Eight Interludes*, 1615)

One other way Cervantes made his first attempt to break into the literary world of Madrid was by writing plays; when he was an old man he claimed that, back in the 1580s, he had written 'twenty or thirty' plays that had been performed with success and had introduced important theatrical innovations to Spanish audiences. Only two survive from this period. The establishment of permanent theatres in the main Spanish cities at that time had created a strong market for plays but the audiences were not yet very discriminating so that anyone capable of knocking together even a mediocre dramatic script could sell his wares. Cervantes, however, convinced himself, as a result of these easy early successes, that he had a vocation as a dramatist and he would spend more than thirty years of his life trying to persuade increasingly sceptical managers that this was so. Cervantes's plays show him overreaching himself in a medium he could not really control; the shortcomings of these works are ones that point up the fact that free-flowing prose narrative or dialogue was his natural instrument of expression. He has little sense of the special kind of selectivity that is needed to construct a dramatic narrative; his inventiveness frequently runs away with him, so that he has too many characters milling about with too little to do, and sub-plots proliferate in an episodic way that obscures the main plot. Cervantes did not have, either, much sense of what constituted, from an actor's point of view, performable speech in verse; one has sympathy with the unnamed manager of a company who, by Cervantes's own account, declared that much could be hoped for from his prose but from his verse nothing. Overdoing things is a general characteristic of Cervantes's full length plays. When audiences became more demanding and a distinctly Spanish dramatic tradition came into being, managers wanted nothing more to do with the kind of plays he wrote. He bitterly resented this and, in *Don Quixote* and elsewhere, mocked the absurdities and illogicalities of the new *comedia* and satirized its creator, Lope de Vega—quite overlooking the fact that his own work hardly measured up to the rationalistic standards he claimed to defend, even allowing for the fact that seventeenth-century views of what was reasonably possible in the theatre were much more liberal then than later. Cervantes got the riposte he ought to have expected when Lope de Vega declared that no one could be so stupid as to admire *Don Quixote*. No objective criteria are likely to persuade the non-specialist reader of today that Cervantes contributes much to dramatic literature. This is a pity because his plays did have a wide-ranging thematic vision, a sense of human destiny and a breadth of imagination that, had they been accompanied by the missing technical ability, might have made him a great and, in Spanish terms, highly original dramatist.

Cervantes's other attempt to win literary fame in the 1580s was represented by his pastoral romance, *La Galatea*, on which he began work soon after his return from captivity. In *Don Quixote* the Priest characterizes pastoral romances as 'books of poems', and *La Galatea* therefore needs to be thought of as part of Cervantes's lifelong obsession with poetry and his desire, against the odds, to achieve recognition as a serious poet. By writing a pastoral romance he presented himself to the reading public as a poet while offering himself a chance to show his paces as a writer of narrative prose too. These romances were the most fashionable form of fictional literature in the Spain of the 1580s. Pastoral romance had begun its life in a small work of genius called *La Arcadia* published in Italian by Jacopo Sannazaro in 1504. This consisted of pastoral or elegiac poems in which shepherds and shepherdesses sang of their experiences of love or, sometimes, of death. Such poetry, traditionally far removed from the realities of peasant life anywhere, involved placing socially important people in an idealized country setting, where they were disguised as shepherds or shepherdesses like the figures in the pastoral eclogues of classical times. The technical novelty of Sannazaro's book was that the poems themselves were now connected by passages of narrative and descriptive prose which, as well as explaining or elaborating on the content of each poem, linked the poems into a narrative whole. The Spanish pastoral romance was created as a development from Sannazaro's book by Jorge de Montemayor's *Diana* (about 1559). It at once secured an enthusiastic reception from European, not just Spanish, readers. The Spanish pastoral romances offered readers a much more formalized and pasteurized vision of the classical world than the *Arcadia* had done. They were also much longer; the love stories told by or about the shepherds and shepherdesses, goatherds, and other pseudo-country-folk in them were both more complex and much more discursive than in their original model; the telling of tales in prose tends to become an end in itself with the poems now often playing a secondary role; a sententious and moralizing tone is much more to the fore and the authors of Spanish pastoral do not hesitate to lecture their readers at length on theories about love, the nature of beauty, the role of fortune in human life and so on. Their prose style is usually slow-moving, melodic, plentifully equipped with descriptive adjectives but slightly and deliberately out of focus, so that the switches from prose to poetry and back again do not jar.

Cervantes's attempt at the pastoral in *La Galatea* was not very successful. The main trouble was the quality of its poetry. Cervantes's poetic inspiration was thin and he was not up to producing the great quantity of pastoral and lyric poetry the genre required of an author. When writing serious poetry, Cervantes was over-ready to settle for simply reproducing traditional clichés; in this way his poetic style differs markedly from his prose style, for one of his special gifts as a prose writer is his constant reaching for the unexpected term, association or metaphor.

La Galatea nevertheless has features of interest to admirers of *Don Quixote*. Cervantes already reveals himself there as an author who is not content to accept a literary model as he finds it. Thus he substitutes the linear narrative technique of previous Spanish pastoral writers by what is known as 'interlacing'—that is, instead of narrating each story from beginning to end, he interrupts the telling of one tale to allow a new one to intervene which, in its turn, may be interrupted, perhaps more than once, before the telling is completed. This technique was already much used in some chivalric romances but Cervantes, in *La Galatea* singles out Ariosto, in *Orlando Furioso*, for the latter's masterly use of it. Cervantes also refuses to abide by the convention that pastoral romance must only deal with stories of poetic love. The long tale of two friends, Timbrio and Silverio, for example, moves all over the Mediterranean and allows the author to make literary use of his very unbucolic memories of war and rapine there; near the very beginning of the book, too, the external tranquillity of the pastoral scene is unexpectedly shattered when one shepherd, in a vengeful fury, stabs a rival bloodily to death. There are also occasional signs of an urge to find room for something rather nearer to the realities of rural life than the pastoral tradition allowed. Already, in *La Galatea*, Cervantes discloses a belief that a story-teller must always surprise or astonish readers by unexpected twists in his plots, or unexpected behaviour by his characters. He was always attracted by what critics sometimes called 'the improbable possible'. It is a fundamental aspect of Cervantes's art, much to the fore in *Don Quixote*.

Cervantes's pastoral writing is by no means confined to *La Galatea*: *Don Quixote*, for example, contains several long and carefully written pastoral tales (such as 'The Tale of Grisóstomo and Marcela' and the story called 'Camacho's Wedding'—'Las bodas de Camacho'). Despite an occasional satirical passage at the expense of the pastoral as a travesty of peasant life as it really is, Cervantes was always drawn to the genre. In the famous examination of the books in Don Quixote's library (I.6) a notable tenderness is shown towards the pastoral romances in general, including *La Galatea*.

Though Cervantes, whether in his pastoral romance or in his verse generally, was himself no more than a mediocre poet, it would be very foolish to ignore his belief in the exalted status of poetry. The words of Don Quixote on the subject, quoted at the beginning of this chapter, are repeated many times in other works. There was nothing unusual about this view of poetry as the supreme literary art; it was a commonplace of Renaissance aesthetic theory. But it presented serious problems to Cervantes. It forced him, as he once said, to struggle 'to make it seem that I possess the gift of poetry that heaven did not give me'; to have abandoned the attempt would have meant, in terms of what he and his contemporaries thought, admitting that the highest form of the art of literature was beyond him. Rather late in life he discovered that the theorists did, in fact, offer him a solution: an epic poem, they explained, could be written perfectly well in prose—it was all a question of the subject and the way it was treated. Out of this discovery came Cervantes's extraordinary last book, *Persiles and Sigismunda*.

Cervantes's own life in the 1580s and later was certainly far removed from that of the leisured, love-lorn, pseudo-rustics he mostly portrayed in *La Galatea*. In 1584 he had a daughter, Isabel, by a married woman, the wife of a street biscuit-maker. Later in the same year he married a country girl eighteen years younger than himself. She lived in the village of Esquivias, a place half-way between Madrid and Toledo, and had a little property there. The couple, who never had any children, were destined to spend years far apart while Miguel earned a living in Andalusia working for the king and his wife looked after her small farm. Their relations seem, however, to have been amicable enough and, when opportunity allowed, normally conjugal. Cervantes visited Esquivias from time to time. There are some suggestive similarities between the names, social affiliations, and the jobs of some of the inhabitants of Esquivias at this time and those of the village characters in *Don Quixote*.

By 1587 Cervantes had realized that, at the age of forty and married, he could not go on living in Madrid with no regular occupation. In that year we find him already working in Andalusia as a commissary (*comisario*) charged with the task of collecting from the small towns and villages of the region the cereals, olive oil, and other agricultural products assessed as their contribution to the supplies needed for the great Armada then fitting out for the expedition against England. After the departure of the Armada, Cervantes continued to work as a royal tax-collector in the Andalusian countryside and remained doing this job until the commissary system was abandoned in 1594. The status of crown commissary was one of some bureaucratic prestige.

The records show that, from the start, Cervantes ran into serious trouble with the town and ecclesiastical authorities with whom he had to deal. At least once he was thrown into a local gaol because he allegedly exceeded his powers; he also got excommunicated for seizing, it was said, immune goods belonging to the church. His chief in Seville defended him and, despite his unpopularity (or perhaps because of it), he retained his post. The documents suggest that Cervantes as a tax-collector was not tactful in handling what was always an unpopular and difficult task. Needless to say the whole *comisario* organization was corrupt and, in 1592, some of those who had been Cervantes's superiors were tried and hanged for embezzling crown property. He himself made a mess of his accounts and was evidently suspected for a time by the royal auditors of having indulged in peculation too. He was arrested in Seville in 1597 and spent thirteen months in the royal prison there before securing his release. His imprisonment was an important event in literary history for, as he explains clearly enough in the Prologue to Part I of *Don Quixote*, that book was conceived in gaol. Through Cervantes saw the inside of Spanish prisons more than once while in Andalusia there is every reason to suppose that it was during his Seville incarceration in 1597–8 that he began work on his famous book. That Cervantes was more incompetent than any tax-collector ought to be in handling and accounting for the goods and money for which he was responsible seems beyond doubt; the bureaucrats in the royal treasury pursued him for years to try to make him straighten things out to their satisfaction.

Cervantes in 1604 spoke of the twenty years since he had published *La Galatea* as his years of unnoticed silence. In terms of published work that was of course true. But it was not entirely correct as a statement about his writing. He had continued to write the occasional play or at least to sign contracts with managers in Seville promising to do so. At the very end of the century, when he was still living there, he probably wrote some of the short stories that would eventually appear collectively in print in 1613. But the real significance of these years when he endlessly travelled round southern Spain as a tax-collector is that, without them, *Don Quixote* could not have been written. This was an age when literature was largely urban in outlook, even when, as in the pastoral, it pretended to be rustic. *Don Quixote* is, except for the Barcelona episodes at the end of Part II, a story of country folk. Its characters, more often than not, are people leading the kinds of lives that Cervantes had come to know while travelling on the king's business. Country life is, though, rarely described deliberately as an exercise in the picturesque or as social comment; it usually simply emerges obliquely as a necessary background to the action. Essential to the plot are the roadside inns of Spain which Cervantes knew so well, inns notorious among European travellers for their lack of comfort and their surly, cheating landlords. They were, nevertheless, the only places of social convergence in the empty Spanish countryside. Here all sorts and classes of travellers found themselves temporarily in close propinquity, offering a natural setting for comical misadventures, romantic adventures, comic and serious conversations, and the telling of tales. Cervantes was the first writer to exploit systematically the varied literary possibilities of the roadside inn.

But, though the fact is less apparent in *Don Quixote* than in some of his short stories and other works, Cervantes during these years also learnt to know well another kind of social milieu—that of the thieves, prostitutes, bully boys, pimps, and cut-throats who notoriously roamed Seville and the other cities of Andalusia. His writings about them not only show that he had closely observed their manner of life and speech; more unusually, he adopts an attitude of wryly amused tolerance towards the criminal classes in general, even when he affects to be disapproving.

In 1604, when *Don Quixote* Part I was in the press, Cervantes set up house in Valladolid, then the Spanish capital. With him he had his wife, two of his sisters, a niece, and his wayward illegitimate daughter. He was still poor and, even at the moment of his greatest literary success, dogged by unsavoury accusations against the women of his household.

The rest is soon told. Shortly after the publication of *Don Quixote* Cervantes moved to Madrid and lived there with his wife for the rest of his life. *Don Quixote* Part I brought him, as we have seen, many readers, outside and inside Spain. But, as he had sold his rights to his publisher, he did not gain financially from its success. The Duke of Béjar, to whom he had dedicated the book in the hope of securing patronage and financial help, proved quite unresponsive; he, perhaps, liked reading chivalric romances or did not like what seemed to be an indirect send-up of the aristocratic values which reading them was believed to encourage. Cervantes did, however, in his final years, secure important patronage. One of his patrons was the powerful Count of Lemos, who was appointed Viceroy of Naples in 1610. The count is the dedicatee of the posthumously published *Labours of Persiles and Sigismunda* as well as of two other books in addition to *Don Quixote* Part II. Another rather unexpected patron at this time was the Archbishop of Toledo, Bernardo de Sandoval y Rojas, nephew of Spain's strong man under Philip III, the Duke of Lerma. He, too, is effusively praised for his charity in the preliminaries to Part II. Thanks to their donations Cervantes was at last able to devote himself to literary work. But he still did not get the acceptance from fellow authors he thought he deserved; in *A Voyage to Parnassus* (1614), he claimed that envy and ignorance denied him the recognition and rewards he knew were his due. A new blow fell in 1614, just when he was completing Part II of *Don Quixote* and hoping to repeat the success of Part I. In that year a work describing itself as the 'Second Part' of the knight's history appeared under a pseudonym. Its author has never been successfully identified but we know that he was an admirer of Lope de Vega and that he considered himself personally to have been held up to scorn in Part I of *Don Quixote*—in which role is unknown. Cervantes was, in fact, rather neatly hoist by his own petard: it was the custom for the romances of chivalry to be continued by authors other than the original one and he had unwisely parodied the tradition by ending Part I with a quotation from *Orlando Furioso* suggesting that someone else might continue the story of *Don Quixote*—a suggestion he had no intention should be taken seriously. To make his punitive intentions clear, the author of the spurious Second Part, in his prologue, made a savage personal attack on Cervantes, calling him, among other things, old, discontented, envious, and friendless. The obsessive references to the interloping Second Part in the final chapters of Cervantes's own Part II and in his Prologue to it reveal the personal bitterness this event caused him, though his creative sense of the comic made it possible for him, in the book itself, to turn the existence of the interloper to positive use in quite unexpected ways.

Cervantes died in Madrid, probably of dropsy, on 23 April 1616. His last surviving written words are to be found in the dedication and the prologue to *The Labours of Persiles and Sigismunda*, the former written just a day or two before his death, 'with one foot already in the stirrup and the fear of death upon me' as he put it then. In the prologue to that serious prose romance Cervantes, significantly, elected to take his leave of the world with a black joke, telling his friends casually that he hoped soon to see them again in the next world. Cervantes had joined a Franciscan lay brotherhood in his later days. He was buried in the Franciscan habit in the church of a nearby convent of Trinitarian nuns. The grave still existed when his long-suffering wife died ten years later for she was buried alongside him, but any trace of it was lost when the church was rebuilt at the end of the century. All the signs are that, even in death, the literary establishment still firmly refused to recognize his genius though, by now, it was quite well known that outside Spain he was regarded as a leading

Spanish writer of the age. His widow saw *Persiles and Sigismunda* through the complicated bureaucratic procedures which publishing a book in Spain then involved but she could only get two little-known poets to write the customary complimentary poems about the author and his work that, in those days, were routinely included among the introductory pages of most new books. Cervantes himself believed, as we have seen, that he was the victim of literary enmities and jealousy. This may be so but it also seems likely that, in the conservative world of Spanish letters at that time, his disconcerting originality as a writer, his failute to follow conventional literary practices and, one suspects, his obvious conviction about his own genius caused him to be regarded as a maverick and an object of suspicion. In our own times some Cervantine specialists have made determined efforts to rehabilitate him as dramatist and poet, claiming that any suggestion that so great a genius failed in any genre must be due to incomprehension on the critic's part rather than to deficiencies in Cervantes's work. I prefer the verdicts of his contemporaries, seconded as they are by the ironically honest admissions of the author himself.

3 The parodying of chivalric romance

'This book of yours has no need of any of those things you say it lacks for the whole of it is an invective against the chivalry books, which Aristotle forgot about, which St Basil never mentioned and which Cicero never came across.' (comment attributed to the author's 'friend' in *Don Quixote* I, Prologue)

My only wish has been to make men hate the fictitious and nonsensical stories found in the books of chivalry which, because of the history of my true Don Quixote, are already tottering and, there is no doubt, will soon collapse altogether. Farewell. (closing words of *Don Quixote* II)

Declarations such as those quoted above about the author's intention in writing *Don Quixote* have sometimes led critics to suppose that Cervantes's driving motive, when he wrote both parts of his most famous book, really was an aesthetic and moral one: the destruction, on artistic and ethical grounds, of the extraordinary compulsion to read chivalric romance that had characterized sixteenth-century European readers. However, when we look at his attitudes to the romances more closely, it is apparent that he was, at the very least, much more ambivalent about them than these formal statements of intention suggest. Indeed we may come even to doubt whether they are much more than a handy cover behind which he could devote himself creatively, not negatively, to what really interested him about the romances: the opportunity they gave him for extended parody. It is important to recognize and understand the ambiguity of Cervantes's approach to the romances because his equivocal stance is, perhaps more than anything else, the factor which gives *Don Quixote* its depth and its subtlety.

The first thing to note is that Cervantes's proclaimed purpose involved, even by 1605, flogging a horse that was anyway nearly dead. In Spain, though not elsewhere, the vogue of the chivalry books had been in a fast decline since at least the 1580s. The last new romance ever written there was printed in 1602 and reprints of the older ones had by that time become rare. His suggestion quoted above, that, as late as 1615, when Part II was published, these works still needed treating as a menace to good taste is clearly an absurd one. The second point to observe is that Cervantes himself had plainly been, at least until quite near the time he began to write *Don Quixote* in the 1590s, a voracious and enthusiastic reader of many of the forty or so separate romances published in sixteenth-century Spain. Evidence for Cervantes's extensive reading of them is not only to be found in the way he refers to many of them by title and then discusses them or parodies material in them; it has been shown that other adventures and situations in his book often originate as reminiscences of romances, sometimes quite obscure ones, which he never mentions by name. The point is important for an understanding of the way Cervantes's first readers must have received his book; many of them were still familiar enough with these works at first-hand for them to respond to the burlesqueing of their contents with an instant discernment that, in the absence of markers, may well elude the modern reader. Thus the comic impact of the work must have been, in this particular way, much stronger in earlier times than it can be today when, indeed, by a paradox that Cervantes, himself such a connoisseur of the paradoxical, would have appreciated, the book he claimed was written to destroy the romances of chivalry has become the main instrument that keeps green the memory of what they are like.

Cervantes's ambiguous approach to the romances can be illustrated in many intratextual ways. The reader of the

Prologue to Part I, having there been led to suppose that the prose romances alone are to be the subject of attack, soon finds, during the short account of Don Quixote's first sally from his village, that the delightful popular ballads on chivalric themes seem to be nearly as much in his mind as the romances are. Cervantes was certainly no enemy of these or any other ballads. Even more unexpected things happen during the scrutiny of the books in Don Quixote's library which follows his first return home (I. 6). This examination, reasonably enough, starts by naming and commenting on his collection of chivalry books. But it soon, inconsequentially, moves on to a discussion of the pastoral romances Don Quixote possesses and then to a commentary on his collection of epic poems on various heroic themes written by sixteenth-century Spanish poets. These works not only have nothing to do with the case we are supposed to be considering; they are often praised by the scrutineers. Matters are made even more confusing by the treatment accorded some of the chivalric romances themselves. Though most of these books, after examination by the Priest and the Barber, are condemned to be burnt (in a bold parody of an inquisitorially sponsored *auto de fe*), we find to our surprise that *Amadis of Gaul*, the earliest, most famous and most imitated of the Spanish romances, is to be saved from the fire because the Barber says that he has heard that it is 'the best of all the books of this kind that have been written'. The Priest had wanted to condemn it to the flames because it was the model for so many others of its kind—a reaction that at least had the merit of consistency. However, he accepts the validity of the Barber's point without demur. Since *Amadis of Gaul* is going to turn out to be the main inspiration of and authority for Don Quixote's actions and thoughts as a knight errant, this praise of it, and its preservation, undermine any pretensions of Cervantes to be a root-and-branch enemy of chivalric romance. The whole episode of the scrutiny of the books offers an excellent example of the way Cervantes, in

Don Quixote, leaves his readers unsure where he really stands. Are we meant to take the views on literature of a village priest and a village barber, together with those of the two women of Don Quixote's household, as those of the author himself? Or, on the contrary, are we to see in their remarks and actions an ironical comment on the way, in sixteenth-century Spain, minor clerics and ignorant laymen and lay women set themselves up as censors of literature? The Priest, we remember, is described as a graduate of the most unprestigious university in Spain—Sigüenza—and the Barber, the text suggests, came to the defence of *Amadis* on hearsay evidence, without apparently having read it himself. The Priest may be in the same case as regards his denunciation of the work; he uses equivocal language on this point.

There are still further complications about the approach of Cervantes's book to chivalric romance. The subject-matter and, more particularly, the style of *Don Quixote* are also considerably influenced by Cervantes's readings of the Italian comic verse epics already mentioned, notably Ariosto's *Orlando Furioso*, finally completed in 1532, a work which, it has been said, showed that the comic can be noble. From it, among other borrowings, he may well have taken the initial idea of making his own knight mad, though there were other precedents for that in traditional chivalric romance. More importantly, perhaps, he borrowed from Ariosto the latter's habit of pulling the carpet from under the feet of his characters in their most exalted or didactic moments. In one of the most famous episodes in *Don Quixote* (I.25–6), the influence of *Orlando Furioso* on the mad knight's fantasies is made clear; Don Quixote decides that, though there is as yet no cause for it, he had better anticipate events and play the role of the grief-stricken lover spurned by his lady—a fate that he knows normally overtakes the heroes of chivalric romance at some time. He is uncertain whether he should imitate the sufferings of Amadis during the latter's self-exile as a rejected lover on the sea-girt Rock of Desolation, or whether, instead, he should go destructively mad, ravaging the countryside single-handed, as Orlando did when he found his lady love Angelica had been sleeping with a Moorish youth, Medoro. Don Quixote cannot see that the latter option implies a parallel insulting to Dulcinea's reputation. In the event, evidently realizing (though he of course does not say so) that his advanced age and his limited strength make it impracticable for him to go about uprooting trees with his bare hands, he decides to imitate Amadis. But the episode places *Orlando Furioso* squarely among the possible targets for Cervantes's parody, though it was a work he venerated.

One more illustration of Cervantes's ambiguous treatment of chivalresque romance needs comment. As the crazed Don Quixote is being escorted home in a cage by the Priest, the Barber, and Sancho, the travellers are joined on the high road by an important man—a canon of Toledo and his escort (I. 47). When the nature of the knight's madness has been explained, the canon proceeds to discourse at length on the literary defects of the prose romances, doing so on a much higher level of discussion than Cervantes usually employs when causing his other characters to denounce them. The canon here uses the kind of theoretical arguments against these works elaborated by sixteenth-century critics who took their cue ultimately from Aristotle's well-known doctrines concerning verisimilitude in literature, the nature of literary forms, and so on. All this at first seems clear enough; Cervantes's objections to the romances of chivalry, voiced by the canon, are well-grounded in terms of contemporary views about what qualities prose fiction needs to have if it is to be respectable. But then the canon unexpectedly proceeds to backtrack. He finds in the romances one admirable feature: the unrestricted field they offer for inventiveness and imagination to spread themselves. Then, despite his previous condemnation of the genre, he goes on to admit that he himself had had a shot at writing a chivalric romance which avoided the faults he had complained of. He had, he smugly observes, written more than a hundred folios of manuscript which had met not only with the approbation of intelligent critics but also of common readers concerned only to hear nonsense read! The canon's exercise in literary punditry on the subject of the romances is thus ironically undermined out of his own mouth. The details the canon gives of this adventure into authorship raise the possibility that we are here dealing with a reminiscence from Cervantes's own autobiography. Had he, perhaps, once partly written, and then abandoned, a chivalry book?

However ambiguous Cervantes's attitudes to the romances may have been, there can be no arguing about the fact that *Don Quixote* is, structurally as well as thematically, a sustained parody of these works. That is to say, Cervantes continually takes the traditional material from which they are made and by displacing it from its proper context into an incongruous one, seeks to make it ridiculous. While it is doubtless possible to enjoy *Don Quixote* without knowing more about chivalric romance than what that book itself has to say, such an approach will scarcely suffice to enable us to understand the kind of impact it had on Cervantes's earlier readers. Parody is by definition unfair to the work parodied so we cannot look to the comic adventures of Don Quixote and Sancho Panza to provide any kind of objective account of what these books were really like; though the knight himself supplies on a number of occasions potted summaries of their contents, these describe them only from his idiosyncratic viewpoint.

The vogue of the romances was a social, not merely a literary phenomenon. Originally, in the Middle Ages, chivalric literature was written for aristocratic readers. Its popularity in sixteenth-century Europe extended its readership, and therefore a familiarity with aristocratic ideals and pretensions, to all who could read or could find someone to read to them; Cervantes, in *Don Quixote*, on a number of occasions, describes the nature of this extended readership. The condemnation of the romances by a whole string of clerical and humanist critics proved quite ineffective; neither the royal censorship nor the inquisitorial censors paid any attention to demands that their circulation in Spain should be prohibited. Nor were the clergy by any means united in condemning them. The clerical censor who in 1602 recommended publication of the very last new chivalric romance ever published there assured the royal council that it was a narrative of praiseworthy and virtuous deeds which provided good models of behaviour for the nobles of Spain to imitate, so inciting them to perform illustrious deeds in the service of king and faith.

The Spanish romances of chivalry have their origins in the epic poetry of medieval France, either that purporting to recall the heroic deeds of the Frankish knights of Charlemagne's times or the legendary tales of Celtic origin involving King Arthur and the Knights of the Round Table. When these stories abandoned their verse form for that of prose in the later Middle Ages they, like their later descendants, remained anchored in the structural and stylistic world of medieval epic poetry. This left them free to portray epic poetry's larger-than-life heroes outside a context of what was possible or probable in everyday terms. The dream-like world of these romances is dominated by knights and ladies whose sole concern is with living by the idealistic, half-religious, medieval laws of chivalry and also by the no less complicated and ritualized doctrines of courtly love that so much attracted and inspired Renaissance as well as medieval poets. No other concerns or duties usually trouble their single-minded dedication to the pursuit of chivalric fame and perfect love. The knight's life in the romances is one long testing by ordeal in which he continually seeks to establish his prowess as knight and lover, as Don Quixote, too, does. Sometimes he proves his heroism and chivalry by fighting in the armies of his sovereign but, more often, he wanders the world alone with his squire (hence the term knight errant), seeking for opportunities to prove himself in single combat against other knights, against giants (usually symbols of evil in the romances) or against other traditional symbolic creatures like dragons, serpents, and the like. Also ranged against him are powerful enchanters, male and female. These are by far the most dangerous of his enemies because they have the power to use their magic both to render the knight militarily impotent and, by changing the appearance of things and people, to deceive and entrap him. Much use is made, too, of the fact that the lowered visor of a knight in armour made it impossible for his opponent to recognize him. This inability to see an opponent's face in combat is exploited twice in key situations in Cervantes's book.

The other ordeal the knight must continually undergo is his trial by courtly love. The code demands of him heroic self-control and patience. As lover he must adopt the role of humble vassal of the lady he has chosen. From her, coldness, unfairness, and apparent rejection are required, all of which the knight has to bear patiently and without resentment since the goddess-like creature he adores must be deemed by him incapable of error. Love is thus a constant source of pain to him, but it is a pain that masochistically gives him pleasure since the more deeply he suffers, the greater must be his love. It is easy to understand why sixteenth-century women readers, accustomed in their daily lives to being treated as inferiors to men, were, according to contemporary critics, such avid readers of the romances. Of course not all the knights managed, or even tried, to be such perfect lovers as Amadis was. Some, like their ladies, were depicted as falling more or less easily into uncourtly sexual ways. Their weakness served to set off the greater achievement of the truly courteous heroes or, perhaps, also simply to prevent an excess of perfection boring the reader.

A special convention of the romances was that their real authors nearly always claimed to have done no more than reproduce in Spanish translation a genuinely historical narrative originally written down in remote times by an obscure foreign chronicler in his own language. Cervantes, in *Don Quixote*, was to go in for a great deal of complicated teasing of the reader by parodying this convention. The romances, also, took great care to avoid localizing the actions they described in any recognizable geographical milieu, for to do so would inevitably be an upsetting intrusion into their secluded world of the imagination, diminishing and de-activating it by unwelcome contact with verifiable reality. This is a convention that Cervantes cannot imitate in *Don Quixote* in respect of the knight's real journeyings but his awareness of it is perhaps responsible for his deliberate failure to give a name to his hero's village in the opening sentence of the book. To it is also due his great caution about using any geographical names at all and the way in which, until near the end of Part II, he carefully keeps Don Quixote and Sancho out of towns and cities. It is no accident that, on the one occasion when he breaks this rule—the visit to Barcelona—plausibility is lost.

In the romances a variety of devices—magic ships and boats, flying horses, and transporter spells—are used as part of the normal order of things to eliminate the restraints of distance and to move the characters with great speed from one country, or one continent, to another. While this characteristic again cannot be re-enacted as direct parody in *Don Quixote*, where all the characters are, of course, restricted to the means of locomotion available in Cervantes's time, it is frequently and hopefully present in Don Quixote's mind and, in Part II, the knight's belief in the ready availability to him of the supernatural forms of transport described above is used during the pair's long stay in the palace of the Duke and Duchess to make plausible some of the burlesque tricks which their host and hostess play on them.

It remains for us to consider, in the present chapter, how Cervantes sets about his parody of the books of chivalry. Parody was, of course, in his time a frequently used if not highly regarded literary form. It was usually motivated by dislike or anger—against a literary fashion, a fellow author and so on. Such parodies were intended to hurt by ridicule and were usually content to operate on an uncomplicated level. Parody does not, though, need to be motivated by hostility. As the fondness of the Middle Ages for religious parody shows, parody may have only a scant negative intent, being more concerned with amusing by displacing well-known and respected material from its familiar context. Despite his suggestions that he had been moved to write *Don Quixote* because of his dislike of the romances, Cervantes's parody belongs to the latter category.

The work certainly fulfils one of the essential requirements of parody and, perhaps, of most comic literature. It is conceived as a conspiracy between author and readers against the characters who appear in the book and, most particularly of course, against Don Quixote himself. The author promises his readers opportunities, through the mechanisms of parody, for laughter at the expense of his characters. With this result should go the comfortable sense of superiority that such laughter brings to those who laugh. The promise is, indeed, very frequently redeemed. But Cervantes always found it hard not to subvert established literary conventions and he was not content to accept the conventions of parody as he found them. He soon sets about tampering with the traditional pattern of this comic form by manipulating its boundaries. Thus, at various times, and increasingly as the novel progresses, Don Quixote and Sancho, as well as a number of the other characters, are shown in a guise which leaves the reader uncertain about who, in fact, is superior to whom: is it really himself, or have the supposedly comical characters in the book managed to seize for the moment the position that, by the traditions of parody, should be his?

Cervantes, as parodist, is an unreliable conspirator for his readers to get along with.

The basis of the parody in *Don Quixote* is, of course, the confrontation between the imaginary world of the romances and the everyday world the book's readers are familiar with. The mechanism which makes this confrontation possible is the madness of Don Quixote himself; he lives physically in the real world but believes, as a result of his malady, that he can, at will, step from it into the world of the romances, so making this conterminous with the real world. The madness of Don Quixote needs to be discussed in a separate chapter. Suffice it to note here that his insanity does not just make him believe that the books of chivalry portray a past historical reality that he can enter and cause to come alive again: these books have taken control of his mind, programming it so that he must always turn to them for instruction, explanations, and reassurance, or to cite their authority to confound his critics. In this respect he is a kind of automaton powered entirely by literature.

A key feature of Don Quixote is his inauthenticity—the fact that he is, physically as well as socially, lacking in the essential qualities of the literary heroes whose company he sets out to join. His exasperated niece, towards the beginning of Part II, tries to make him comprehend this when she says

> 'you want to be thought a fighting man, though you are old; strong, though you are infirm; that you can straighten out wrongs, being yourself bent by the years; and worst of all, you pretend that you are a knight when you are not one . . .' (II. 6)

Don Quixote, making no attempt to refute his niece's points, typically responds with a flood of irrelevant sententious eloquence about genealogies and pedigrees, riches and poverty; the niece does not understand that it is useless to try to argue a madman out of his mania by rational discourse. She is right, though, to draw attention to Don Quixote's physical and social disabilities. His physical incompetence to play the role of a hero from the chivalry books is directly responsible for many of the humiliating disasters that befall him; the fact that he is only a fake knight (*caballero*) means that he can be treated as an object of derision with impunity by all and sundry. These defects make it inevitable that crude burlesque, even after the first sally, will always play a prominent part in the parody.

Sancho Panza, similarly, is without any of the qualities that would make him a plausible squire. In the romances, as in the real world of the Middle Ages, a squire is by definition a youth of gentle birth and education who is serving his apprenticeship as a knight by attending on one who has already been received into the order of chivalry. Sancho is a peasant neighbour of Don Quixote, married, with children, and illiterate. When Cervantes invented him he seems to have had in mind Gandalín, the rather pert squire of Amadis. Don Quixote succeeds in getting Sancho to accompany him by appealing to the latter's peasant greed with the unlikely promise of the governorship of an island. It is worth observing, however, that Don Quixote stops short of thinking that Sancho, whom he has known as a neighbour for some time, has been metamorphosed into a real squire. He simply hopes the rustic, despite his innate foolishness, will learn to behave like the real thing. Sancho, therefore, while partly functioning in the book as a kind of lower-class travesty of his master, is at the same time an instrument by which the latter maintains a sporadic toehold on the world of the sane. As for Sancho himself, he is disposed, or half-disposed, to accept Don Quixote's chivalric world, despite the accumulated unpromising evidence of his senses; only if that world is real can his ambition to be a governor come true.

There is, of course, no precedent in the romances for the

lengthy conversations between knight and squire about the experiences they have together and about many other things. Cervantes was fully aware of the way these conversations, which contribute so largely to the originality of the book, represent a departure from the romance pattern. To make sure the reader also realizes it he draws attention to the matter in Part I. 20, where Don Quixote complains that, though he has read an infinite number of books of chivalry, he has never come across in them any squire as garrulous or as impertinent as Sancho; he could have added, nor any knight as talkative as himself.

Cervantes's parody thus rests largely on its redeployment of episodes, themes, and characters borrowed from the romances. Among the borrowings special stress needs to be put on the vital role played by the figure of the evil-intentioned enchanter in making the parody work. Confronted, as Don Quixote constantly is, by the fact that what he sees, or thinks he ought to be seeing, does not appear that way to others, he finds in the figure of the unseen but malevolent wizard ready-made explanation that enables him to keep his delusions not only intact but rationally accounted for: if a castle looks like an inn or a giant like a windmill, or Dulcinea like a peasant girl, it is because these enemies have tampered with the appearance of things in order to deceive or frustrate him. The stylistic characteristics of the romances are, of course, also parodied. These works, for example, made a point of using archaic phonetical forms and archaic expressions to convey an impression of their supposedly ancient origins; Cervantes makes good use of this feature for comic purposes by causing Don Quixote, if only sporadically, to speak incongruously like a figure from a much earlier time.

Structurally Cervantes's book follows its chivalric model fairly closely. Don Quixote and Sancho are engaged on a seemingly endless journey towards an uncertain destination, as are the heroes of the chivalry books. The essence of the book, similarly, lies in the adventures that happen unexpectedly to them on the way. In the romances, though, the adventures recounted are not usually only those of the knight whose name is given in the title; much space is usually allowed for recounting the deeds of various other knights. Cervantes could not imitate this practice because the nature of his parody prevented it; there could not be more than one Don Quixote. As a result the main weight of the narrative has to be carried by the knight and his squire. It has been calculated that more than 500 characters appear in the pages of the work; while a few of these play important minor parts, it is always plain that the action, except in the extraneous interpolated stories, centres round Don Quixote and Sancho.

Any serious study of Cervantes's book, it will be seen, must start from the fact that it was conceived by its author as an extended parody of the romances of chivalry. But it is a parody written by a man who, despite what he alleges, still responds emotionally, though no longer intellectually, to the ideals and the assumptions to be found in these works.

4 What happens in *Don Quixote*: Part I

'Now,' said Don Quixote, 'I declare that the author of my story [Part I] was no sage but some ignorant chatterer who set himself to write it gropingly, without any rational method, letting it come out anyhow, like Orbaneja, the painter of Úbeda, who, when they asked him what it was he was painting, replied: "Whatever it turns out to be." ' (*Don Quixote* II. 3)

Set against what we now expect from the modern novel, the story-line in both parts of *Don Quixote* is weakly drawn. To a considerable extent this is due to the parodic nature of the enterprise; chivalric romance depended on a succession of chance adventures, so Cervantes must follow a similar pattern. What happens to the knight and his squire does not therefore follow any methodical or tight-knit plan. The spatial movement of master and man along the roads of Spain is what keeps the plot moving forward. The story-line is also further weakened, specially in Part I, by the interpolation of a number of extraneous stories from which comic purpose is absent and in which Don Quixote and Sancho play at most only a secondary part. There is quite a lot of reference back to experiences the two have had but very little sign of close forward planning by the author. One of the charms of the book, indeed, is that what happens in it has the desultory quality of life itself. There is sporadic modification of the characters of knight and squire, more markedly in Part II, but even there this development is not consistently maintained; if Cervantes's immediate comic purpose requires it, Don Quixote may be made without comment to revert to the condition of total madness and Sancho to that of unredeemed simpleton in which they first appear.

The adventures themselves, like those in chivalric romance proper, tend to be repetitive and ritualistic in their form, involving, as they do, the confrontation of Don Quixote's hallucinatory chivalric world, entirely fed by literary reminiscence, with the realities others see. The narrative structure is, however, much looser and fortuitous than it is even in the romances, where, despite all the complexities of the interlaced method of narration, the author of, say, *Amadis of Gaul* usually manages to retain a fairly tight grip on plot and sub-plots. As is the norm in parody, Cervantes gives the pursuit of comic effect priority over considerations of formal ordering and coherence. In Cervantes's own time it was pointed out that there were, in Part I, a number of inconsistencies, contradictions, and narrative omissions which suggest that he did not closely revise anything he had written, and give ironic point to the quotation at the beginning of this chapter. But we cannot be sure that these apparent 'slips' had always passed by unnoticed; setting up deliberate ambiguities and conundrums is part of Cervantes's stock-in-trade in this book, as is his desire to subvert the notion that everything has a fixed and certain identity. Certainly, in Part II, he would, instead of apologizing for the slips in Part I to which readers had drawn attention, set about extracting new teasing effects from their presence.

The Prologue to Part I

The Prologue, written in 1604 after the final completion then of the text proper, soon turns, as Cervantes's prologues often did, into a piece of pseudo-autobiographical fiction in its own right. This one also is (from its ironical opening words directed to the 'idle reader') a parody of the customary author's address to the reader as used by Spanish writers at this time. Instead of the posture of hopeful self-depreciation that conventionally characterized such writing, Cervantes tells his readers that he does not care what they say about his book, good or bad.

The end of the Prologue, as we have already seen, asserts the alleged aesthetic and moral purpose of the book: the destruction of chivalric romance. It also contains an important statement about the effects the author (here through an *alter ego*, the imaginary 'friend') intends the work to have on its readers:

> Labour also so that, when he reads your story, the melancholic is moved to laughter, the happy man to laugh still more, judicious people marvel at its inventiveness, the unschooled are not affronted, the solemn ones do not despise it, nor the prudent fail to applaud it.

It will be noted that the comic purpose of the book is given pride of place twice in this schedule.

Part I: the first sally

Chapters 1 to 5 deal with the first sally of Don Quixote. On this journey the knight travels alone on his broken-down nag. The animal, in accordance with a tradition about a hero's horse found in some forms of chivalresque literature, he names 'Rocinante'; the name is a burlesque one which brings together the Spanish word *rocín* ('a broken-down horse') and the Spanish term for a knight errant, *caballero andante*. Rocinante, henceforth inseparable from Don Quixote, of whom he is a kind of dumb *alter ego*, is one of the important characters in the book, just as Sancho's ass, when the squire joins Don Quixote, will function as a sort of more or less silent mirror-image of the peasant.

Cervantes describes in considerable detail in Chapter I the visual appearance of the future Don Quixote as well as his life-style and household. He is a typical impoverished rural gentleman, aged about fifty, lean-faced, and of a generally dried-up appearance. In the opening sentence of the book, as already mentioned, Cervantes deliberately fails to name the village where his hero lives. All we are told is that it is in the extensive region of open plainlands in southeastern central Spain known as La Mancha, a region well-known to the author because of his journeys as royal commissary. Cervantes's deliberate planting of ambiguities again comes into play when he refers to his gentleman's real surname; he mentions three possible ones (all with comic implications) that have been proposed but declares himself uncertain which was correct. The name his middle-aged gentleman chooses for himself in his role of knight errant represents a rather complex concatenation of meanings. The name 'Quixote' (*quijote* in Spanish alludes to the English *cuisse*, the piece of armour that protects the front of the thigh) is in itself a ludicrous choice, possibly with sexual overtones in Cervantes's time. The suffix *-ote* has a potentially derisive implication in Spanish, too. The would-be knight, however, probably also had it in mind to compare himself to the Sir Lancelot of the Arthurian tales (*Lanzarote* in Spanish). At least to the first generations of Cervantes's Spanish readers, the very name of his hero thus must have seemed wholly comical.

Don Quixote's household is a very modest one for the times, consisting of a housekeeper of over forty and an unaccounted-for niece of under twenty. Neither in Chapter I nor anywhere else in the book are we told anything about Don Quixote's life before we first come across him. The omission is not borrowed from the romances of chivalry, which were keen on genealogies, and is plainly deliberate. It is an omission that had important consequences; the absence of any data about Don Quixote's biography before the period of his life covered by the book has been an important factor in allowing him to be turned into a mythical personage who can lead an existence outside it. It also allows Cervantes to attribute to him, without having to account for them historically, whatever knowledge or views he wishes.

The Don Quixote of the first sally is a ridiculous figure who creates situations which move from uncompromising burlesque into crude, knockabout farce and back again.

Nevertheless the first sally already sets the pattern for the sorts of events in which he will be involved for the rest of the book. It establishes the kinds of effects which contact with him will have on others. It also points up the underlying topic which the work will continuously exploit for strictly artistic purposes—the complexities involved in the confrontation between 'reality' as sane folk perceive it and the appearances that the hallucinations of the insane can impose on it.

The self-proclaimed 'Don Quixote de la Mancha' sets out on his first journey as a knight errant on a summer's morning, riding on Rocinante and decked out in rusty armour and a crudely patched-up half-cardboard headpiece. He had already chosen, as the noble lady every knight errant must love and be constantly inspired by, a peasant girl from a neighbouring village. She is called Aldonza Lorenzo, but Don Quixote renames her Dulcinea del Toboso. By the second sally he will have mostly forgotten Dulcinea's peasant origins.

The opening adventure in the book occurs when Don Quixote comes upon the first of the various roadside inns where so much of the action of the book is located. He has never been formally dubbed a knight and, to put this right, the first example of a complex parody of the chivalry books takes place at the inn, where the ceremony of his admission to the order of chivalry is arranged. Don Quixote believes the inn to be a castle, the picaresque innkeeper to be its noble captain and two travelling whores he sees outside the door to be beautiful ladies of rank resident in the castle. He asks the innkeeper, in his supposed role as knight-castellan, to conduct the required ceremony, addressing him in the courtly, archaic language used in the chivalry books. The innkeeper, realizing he has to do with a madman, is the first of many characters in Cervantes's book who, simply to have some fun at Don Quixote's expense, decide to play up to the *soi-disant* knight's hallucinations by acting out the role thrust upon them. In a burlesque ceremony which has everyone else in stitches of laughter, Don Quixote is duly knighted. The tables, as so often, are turned when the new 'knight' declines to pay for his keep, pointing out that, in the chivalry books, there is no record of any knight handling money. He is less lucky with some muleteers staying at the inn, one of whom he attacks believing him to be a knight who has insulted him. This episode leads to his getting the first of the many stonings he will suffer in the book. In another adventure, he interrupts and rebukes a farmer who is beating his hired boy. Don Quixote believes that in doing so he is performing his chivalrous duty of going to the defence of the weak, but the reader sees how the madman's good-intentioned interference only, in the end, makes matters worse. The final adventure on the first sally occurs when he holds up a party of travelling silk merchants on the king's highway demanding, in the mode of the chivalry books, that they acknowledge Dulcinea, on pain of attack, to be the most beautiful maiden in the world. Finding their reply unsatisfactory, Don Quixote charges the merchants in one of those accesses of choler to which he is prone but Rocinante, unaccustomed to such activity, falls and throws him. A servant of the merchants then beats him severely, a misfortune that he attributes to the ill-will of highway robbers. Because of the comic contexts in which Don Quixote continually gets beaten up or otherwise hurt in the book we are liable to overlook the amount of physical violence that actually takes place in it, though, like violence in traditional theatrical farce, the effects of the hurt done, however grave, last no longer than the author wishes them to. On this occasion, still firmly believing himself to be living in the world of literary fiction, Don Quixote is rescued by a kindly neighbour from his village and carried home on the back of a donkey. He had been away three days.

The second sally

The book-burning and other methods by which the Priest,

the Barber and the women of the household try to cut him off from the immediate source of his madness have already been described. These are unsuccessful and, after a fortnight, the knight, accompanied now by his 'squire', Sancho Panza, departs secretly by night on his second sally (I.7). The introduction of Sancho Panza, an introduction justified in terms of the knight errant–squire relationship in the romances, was, as he used it, a stroke of genius on Cervantes's part. It made possible the continuous conversations between the two men that turn a burlesque with limited possibilities into an in-depth comic study of a confrontation between intelligent madness and perspicacious ignorance. Sancho is described, when he first appears, as a man with very little sense in his pate. His initial role is to point up Don Quixote's hallucinatory vision of the world by interpreting it in terms of his own stolidly down-to-earth response to sense impressions. But this is not what he intends. He wants to believe that the fictional world of chivalric romance which Don Quixote describes to him is really there. His problem is that he never contrives, at least in Part I, to see it.

Cervantes, finding Sancho growing in potential and importance to the story as it proceeds, improvises new traits for him. The constant use of popular proverbs, which we now think of as a special feature of Sancho's speech, is not in fact introduced until chapter 19. At about the same time, conscious now of the increased depth and subtlety to be gained by making Sancho less totally stupid than he had originally painted him, Cervantes hit on the idea of making the peasant an attentive listener to sermons from which, though illiterate, he had supposedly contrived to pick up a good deal of information and doctrine which enables him to argue at times on something like level terms with his master. Constant contact with Don Quixote on their journeying causes him, even in Part I, to pick up, for example, his master's archaic speech. Soon, too, he becomes able to discuss, to comic effect, the contents, as he imagines them, of the chivalry books he hears Don Quixote ceaselessly talking about. Contact with Sancho has its effect on the knight, too—most obviously, in that he starts to lard his carefully polite discourse with popular proverbs.

From the time of the squire's entry into the book his behaviour, notions, and speech are liable to strike others as just as unexpected and comical as those of his master; as well as exhibiting in general terms the natural folly and cunning of peasants in literature that was traditionally expected of him, Sancho is constantly beset by his need to try to reconcile the knight's chivalric hallucinations and the world as he himself perceives it to be. Towards the end of Part I, Cervantes draws the reader's attention to the fact that Sancho by now is, as a result, nearly as mad as his master (I.46). Equally there are signs that Don Quixote is, unwittingly, sometimes influenced by Sancho's ceaseless questioning of the veracity of his hallucinations. He may now surprise us by not taking every roadside inn to be a castle or by admitting that he made a mistake when he took a simple funeral procession met with on the high road to herald the kind of adventure to be found in the chivalry books that required him to take a knight errant's action.

Certain features of Sancho's character, however, do not change. He always remains a coward, a glutton, and an instinctive liar. Among the things that do change is his attitude to his master. Having originally only agreed to serve Don Quixote for reasons of greed and ambition, he develops (and will eventually admit to) an affection for the knight. This is an important factor in arousing the reader's sympathy for Don Quixote, or, perhaps more exactly, in allowing the modern reader to feel such sympathy. Sancho's affection survives his growing suspicions (by chapter 18) that Don Quixote, for all his posturing, is a good deal less ready to defend his squire from danger than he ought to be.

The second sally takes up almost the whole of the remainder of Part I. It lasts only about three weeks, though

Cervantes assigns no particular importance to chronology. Most of the adventures are based on commonplace sights or encounters that any travellers on the roads of southern Spain in Cervantes's time would expect to find: a group of windmills, a lady in a carriage on her way to Seville, a party of Benedictine monks mounted on mules, goatherds and shepherds attending their flocks, a group of chained prisoners being escorted to a port to become galley slaves, constables of the Santa Hermandad (rural constabulary) going about their duty, a canon of Toledo travelling in style, a religious procession bearing an image of the Virgin, an itinerant barber who has put his barber's basin on his head in a rainstorm, a funeral party escorting a body by night on a bier, and so on. Then there are the lonely roadside inns where Don Quixote and Sancho sometimes put up for the night or for longer periods. The form is nearly always the same: Don Quixote, despite the bewildered protestations of Sancho, usually insists on turning these commonplace travellers' experiences into exciting but hallucinatory ones drawn from his conviction of the reality of chivalric romance and his illusion that he is a genuine knight errant. Fenced off as he is from the real world by his delusions, Don Quixote is a supreme egotist. We must not be misled by his constant talk of succouring the weak and combating evil; only one thing really drives him—his search for chivalric fame that will earn him a romance devoted to his achievements. Even his total devotion to the imaginary Dulcinea is altogether egocentric. But the fame he achieves in Part I is not that he seeks. He becomes, instead, well known in La Mancha and its neighbouring regions as a madman whose antics may amuse some but more frequently annoy others. His attempts to play the knight errant always lead, here as in the first sally, either to his personal humiliation or to harmful results. This would-be do-gooder, because he is mad, always hurts either himself or others. When he performs what to his deluded mind is a chivalrous and morally good act like restoring their freedom

hose sense
oscillate
involved
ctator.
a del
her,
her
re
e

...risoners on their way to the ...ult him and rob him and Sancho. ...s the slightest inclination to spare ...constantly stoned, beaten up, or ...sed at critical moments by Rocinante ...allike his rider, is physically incapable of ...nded of him.

...however, frequently takes a subtler turn than ...summary suggests. As has been mentioned, ...times, to amuse themselves at the knight's expense, ...e other characters will decide to act out the parts he has allotted them. This is very confusing for the simple-minded Sancho who, specially when the dissemblers are persons of rank who presumably know what's what, is forced to question the validity of his own perfectly correct direct perceptions of things. On other occasions people may decide to accept the knight for what he says he is because they regard him as a potentially dangerous madman and it seems safer to humour him than to argue with him. Either way, the result is that he causes sane people to act as if they were mad. Cervantes was the first writer of prose fiction systematically to subvert in this way, as a comic ploy, the stable linkage between appearance and reality. However, he does it by what are essentially no more than a series of literary conjuring tricks; nowhere in the book are the metaphysical implications of the topic explored, or even mentioned. But, sometimes the narrative does, for all that, have certain enigmatic undertones. The reader is bound to agree with Sancho, for instance, that the windmills are windmills, not giants. It is also true, though, that if one is, like Don Quixote, looking expectantly for giants, then windmills can indeed look rather like them. Once one has accepted the fact of Don Quixote's madness one can perceive a kind of reasonableness behind his misreadings of reality. There is, after all, some kind of affinity between a large flock of sheep moving forwards in the distance and a mighty army, seen from afar, slowly advancing across the

plain. Nor is it only the characters in the book w...
of what reality is may be temporarily made to...
disconcertingly. The reader, too, may find himself...
in the game as something more than a superior spe...
We know well enough, for example, that Dulcin...
Toboso is a figure who, in the form the knight imagines...
exists solely in Don Quixote's fantasy. But he describes...
and refers to her part in his life so often that we also...
liable to catch ourselves believing in her existence mo...
than we do in the real but, in practice, much less...
substantive peasant hoyden whom the knight believes to be...
the beautiful damsel of his dreams: every lover, in his own...
way, wants to create, as Don Quixote does, his own
Dulcinea out of his own Aldonza Lorenzo. The role of
Dulcinea becomes still more equivocal when Sancho, in a
singular moment of insight (I.31), suggests to his master
that the kind of selfless love he appears to feel for her is
the sort men should reserve for their feelings towards God.
This at once obliquely introduces a new dimension into
our assessment of the knight's delusions. It is not the
only occasion in the book when Cervantes allows his burlesque to brush against some manifestation of matters
religious.

Neither part of *Don Quixote* restricts itself to the story of
the adventures of the knight and his squire. A substantial
portion of Part I, from chapter 12 onwards, is concerned
with the narration of tales simply interpolated holus-bolus
into the middle of the main plot. There are some six of
these. As stories their purpose is entirely serious. Some
belong to the pastoral story-telling tradition we have
already encountered in *La Galatea*. Others are complicated
tales of unhappy love fabricated in the very factitious
tradition European short-story writers had borrowed from
Italy. Some critics have argued that they are thematically
not as remote from the story of Don Quixote as they seem
to be, but this view seems difficult to defend, at least in
respect of the stories in Part I. All involve moral issues

which Cervantes is, as usual, disinclined to settle definitively for us.

These stories are well-written examples of the Cervantine short story in the romantic mode. Most modern readers no doubt wish that they were not there, or at least, that there were fewer of them. Their contrived plots, reminiscent of the sleight-of-hand solutions favoured by Spanish dramatists writing in the mode of Lope de Vega, and their avoidance of any attempt to present life as subject to the exigencies of the everyday seem nowadays disconcertingly at odds with the comic tone of the rest of the work. However we cannot just wish these tales away for, from Cervantes's point of view, they formed an essential part of his book. He was prepared to admit (II.44) that two of the tales in Part I—that called 'Inexpedient Curiosity' ('El curioso impertinente') and the partly autobiographical 'The Captive Captain'—had perhaps little to do with the main story, but he defended the others as genuinely part of the experiences of Don Quixote and Sancho. His ironical comment that, anyway, they were 'no less agreeable, skilful and *authentic* [my italics] than the main story itself' (I.28) reminds us that writers of fiction in his day had an attitude towards notions of unity of composition and towards what constituted artistic realism that differ from ours. The interpolated stories of *Don Quixote* were in fact for a long time accepted without much complaint. A German Romantic critic even described them in 1800 as sublime examples of the kind of artfully capricious fecundity through which the Romantic genius revealed itself.

The story that perhaps most deserves attention is the lengthy and involved tale of the affairs of two pairs of lovers which we may call 'Cardenio and Dorotea'. This starts in a minor way in chapter 23 and then weaves its way in and out of the main narrative for much of the rest of Part I. It has all the characteristics already referred to but also some others which make it of special interest. Don Quixote confronts in the fastnesses of the Sierra Morena a youth, Cardenio, who, maddened by lost love, is also wandering in the mountains. In chapter 24 the two love-lorn madmen meet. The meeting ends with them quarrelling over a reference in the chivalry books. They will, however, have more profitable encounters subsequently. In this tale the world known to Sancho, the alienated world of Don Quixote's fantasy and the fictional world of betrothal, betrayal and restitution between well-heeled lovers that Cervantes had recourse to when writing short stories all converge with surprising results. Eventually Dorotea affects to transfer herself in to the world of Don Quixote by pretending to be Princess Micomicona, a damsel in distress from Guinea, who needs his help to recover her Black African kingdom from a giant who has usurped it. She is really now in collusion with the Priest and Barber from Don Quixote's village, who have joined the party with a plan to get the knight home by deliberately playing up to his chivalric delusions.

Also marginal to the main tale are two long, carefully constructed monologues delivered by the knight. In these he speaks on well-worn Renaissance topics traditionally discussed among men of letters. The first of these discourses (I.11) is in the literary pastoral vein: Don Quixote, after sharing the rustic supper of some goatherds, treats them to a learned description of the mythical Golden Age. Criticism has tended to overlook the way irony and burlesque are woven into the knight's lecture: the goatherds, not understanding a word, merely listen, stupefied and unreacting; the traditional pastoral description of the lost age when universal peace reigned and men lived without effort on nature's bounty is presented by the knight with unconscious touches of irony. His exaltation of its peace and tranquility is, of course, comically inapt in the mouth of one who never tires of proclaiming that war is his business and who continuously and gratuitously violates the tranquillity of the social scene.

The second monologue takes place much later in the book during dinner before a large company in the particular inn which figures largely in Part I (chapters 37–8). Don Quixote's theme this time is the traditional debate about whether the career of arms is superior to that of letters, or vice versa. He naturally comes down on the side of arms but once again his arguments take the form of a comical paradox. Peace, he explains, is the greatest good man can desire. Since the true object of war is peace, it follows that it is the soldier rather than the man-of-letters who does the greatest good to society! Once again, Cervantes is careful not to free Don Quixote, even momentarily, from his role as a figure of ridicule. His fellow diners go on eating all the time he is talking and, when he has finished, none bothers to follow up what he has had to say.

Towards the end of the book, in the form of a discussion between the canon of Toledo and the Priest about prose fiction in general and the chivalric romances in particular (I.47–8), we have the only attempt in this book to discuss at length the theory of fiction. The nature of the discussion has already been examined in the preceding chapter and its contradictions noted. The discussion has little direct bearing on the kind of discoveries about fiction that Cervantes has been making empirically in his book. Hardly a word is said in it, for example, about comic writing.

The Spanish chivalric romances, as has been mentioned, used a conventional device to persuade audiences of the historical authenticity of their fictional tales; the story, it was claimed, had been found in an old manuscript written down long ago in an ancient language. Antiquity was supposed to explain away improbability. A characteristic example of the convention is to be found in the prologue to *Amadis of Gaul* where we are told that this work's continuation, *Sergas de Esplandián*, was found in a stone tomb beneath the floor of a hermitage in Constantinople and brought to Spain by a Hungarian merchant. It was written on parchment in a script so ancient that it could only be read with difficulty even by those who knew the language in which it was written. Cervantes seems originally to have intended to do no more than parody for simple comic effect this pretence of the writers of romance. In the event, however, the parody here grew in his hands until it assumed a role that far outstripped anything he had originally intended.

Cervantes sets about confusing the issue of authorship from the beginning of Part I. Its opening sentence, with the use of an authorial 'I', seems to make a direct claim that Cervantes himself is the sole author. However we are soon told that there were two authors; their respective roles are not defined. Later, Cervantes has seen, in this notion of twin authorship, larger possibilities that appeal to his sense of fun and his interest in exploiting the fictionality of fiction. In chapter 8, in the middle of a mock epic battle between Don Quixote and an angry Basque squire, he suddenly brings the narrative to a complete stop, declaring that the 'first' author of the history of Don Quixote had reported that he could find nothing more written about the knight's exploits beyond this point. The 'second' author, however, refused to believe that no such records remained. We are told in great detail how this second narrator came across an Arabic manuscript in Toledo and asked a Spanish-speaking Moor there to look at it. The Moor, when he did so, burst out laughing. It was revealed that the manuscript was a continuation of the history of Don Quixote as written by an Arab historian, Cide Hamete Benengeli (the last name is a pun on the Spanish word for 'eggplant'—a favourite Moorish dish). Cervantes, or, at any rate, the second author of the preceding chapters, got the Moor to translate Cide Hamete's work into Spanish, and chapter 9 then immediately returns to continue the battle between Don Quixote and the Basque 'according to the translator'. The rest of the book, Part II as well as Part I, is supposed to be translated from the history of Don Quixote as told by Cide Hamete. The whole question of authorship is by now, on one level, thoroughly confused but, on another, the reader knows quite well that the book's real author, Cervantes, is simply playing games at his expense.

Cervantes, however, presses his parody forward into still more complications. Speaking now as a commentator, he points out that we have to do with a narrative by an Arab. Since Arabs are ready liars and are the enemies of Spaniards, Cide Hamete's account of the story of Don Quixote, he warns us, may not be either truthful or unprejudiced. From time to time the imaginary Arab historian himself also comments on the story he is telling. So does his 'translator'. As if this were not confusing enough, Cervantes or his *alter ego* emerges from time to time to comment on *them*. Cide Hamete, though we never see him, only hear him or hear about him, becomes not only the supposed author of most of *Don Quixote* but also a character in the book he has written.

Plainly more is involved here than a comic send-up of a rather minor convention of chivalric romance. By suggesting to the reader that, in the hands of a different author, a different account of the adventures of Don Quixote and Sancho might have emerged, Cervantes reminds him that prose fiction is not simply history that did not happen to have happened; authors of fiction might dress their stories up as if they were history but, in fact, fiction, unlike history, is whatever an author chooses to make it. Cervantes's treatment of authorship in *Don Quixote* subverts both the traditional authority of an author *vis-à-vis* his readers and the former's claim that an exclusive relationship exists between him and his works.

Part I ends with Don Quixote's humiliating return to his village as a prisoner in the cage borne on an ox-cart in which the Priest and the Barber had contrived to imprison him for his own good in chapter 46. To be forced to ride in a lowly peasant's cart was traditionally a supreme dishonour for a knight in the chivalric romances. Don Quixote, however, is untroubled because he has ready recourse to his usual explanation; his captivity in the cart is not real—all is the work of evil-intentioned enchanters. The book finally ends with an ironic invitation to the reader to give the book the same credence that intelligent men give to the romances of chivalry! These, we have been repeatedly told, are all lies. Cervantine irony never spared even his own best work.

In the concluding paragraphs a number of broad hints seem to be given that Don Quixote will make a third sally. Even his destination then—Saragossa—is named. But Cervantes, always ready to equivocate, carefully avoids committing himself definitively. He quotes some burlesque sonnets said have been intended as epitaphs for the graves of Don Quixote, Dulcinea, Sancho, and Rocinante. These allow him to end Part I on a determinedly comic note but, as they are also used to mock, in passing, credulous antiquarians and the current fashion for setting up literary clubs all over the place, the reader is left uncertain whether or not to believe in these deaths.

5 What happens in *Don Quixote*: Part II

This second part of *Don Quixote* that I offer you is cut by the same craftsman and from the same cloth as the first one. In it I give you Don Quixote made longer and finally dead and buried . . . (*Don Quixote* II, Prologue to the Reader)

Part II was finished in 1614 and published in 1615. As the quotation given above shows, Cervantes presented it to his readers as a straight continuation of the first part, supporting his claim with a suggestion at the beginning of chapter 1 that only about a month had intervened between the events at the end of Part I and those he now started to narrate. Though he is at pains to assert that nothing has changed since Part I, Part II has plainly been influenced, for instance, by the critical comments readers of that part had evidently made, as well as by new insights into his material acquired by the author himself during the ten-year interval. One thing had, however, not changed. Though Cervantes, by 1615, was sixty-seven—an old man by contemporary standards—there is no lessening of his powers in Part II; his inventiveness is as remarkable as ever, his sense of the comic as acute, his irony as good-humouredly sharp and his manipulation of language as many-sided and distinctive as it was in 1605. Gaiety, more than disillusion, is, despite what some have suggested, still the prevailing impression it communicates to the open-minded reader, specially if the latter can read the book in Spanish and pick up the continuing flow of comic and slyly ironic nuances in its style.

One difference between Part II and its predecessor is the greater and more sustained self-confidence of Sancho Panza and the much increased and sometimes independent role he now plays. Another important innovation in Part II is the introduction, in chapter 2, of the young graduate Sansón Carrasco, son of a villager, who has just come home after completing his studies at the University of Salamanca. He is depicted with the physiognomy of a born humorist: his round face, flat nose, and big mouth, says Cervantes, revealed him to be a mischievous young man, fond of jokes and comic tricks. He will play an important part in Part II, both as witty conversationalist, prankster, and good-hearted would-be rescuer of Don Quixote from his malady and its consequences. The earlier roles of the Priest and the Barber are largely taken over by him in Part II.

Sansón is also responsible for bringing Don Quixote the information that will radically change in Part II the view both knight and squire have of themselves: the news that their deeds have been published in a book which is having great success among readers, not only in Spain but abroad as well. In Part I we have seen that Don Quixote was concerned to win such fame as a knight errant as would ensure that he was worthy to deserve a chivalric romance written with himself as its hero. That object he believes from Sansón's account to have been achieved so that, in Part II, he is more concerned with living up to his reputation as a well-known heroic figure who exists both in literature and in life. Sancho, too, is delighted to find himself a principal character in a book. This adds to his burgeoning self-assurance and self-importance. One thing troubles Don Quixote; the discovery that his story, incomprehensibly, was written by a Moor. However there is a paradoxical feature of his reaction to the news that this book about him exists; he questions Sansón closely about its contents; in the course of the actions which now follow he will meet various people who have also read the book and he will proudly admit that he is its hero. Yet he never reads it himself nor does he ever express any desire to do so. Such a posture at first sight seems wholly improbable, given the knight's addiction to reading chivalric romance and his unbridled egotism, but his failure to want to read his own story in fact shows Cervantes's sureness of touch in a difficult situation. Had Don Quixote discovered that he was really portrayed as a ridiculous madman in Part I, the continuation of his adventures along the same pattern as before, which was what the author and his public wanted, would not have been possible.

Not content with having Don Quixote believe that Part I is a different sort of book from the one it really is, so that a false Part I of *Don Quixote* from now on exists in the minds of knight and squire, Cervantes plays further tricks on the reader to show him how nebulous fictional reality is; thus, in chapter 4, when most of Part II is, of course, still unwritten, Sansón reveals that 'the author' is diligently looking for the manuscript containing the supposedly completed full story so that he can publish it without delay.

Don Quixote is in no hurry to set out on his travels this time. Various conversations between knight, squire, and Sansón, mostly about literature, succeed in writing the Salamancan graduate fully into the story. As a sign of the shape of things to come, too, an entire chapter is given up to a comical session between Sancho and his wife, Teresa, a personage who scarcely appears in Part I. Teresa Panza now enters the book as a minor character in the form of a well-observed village housewife of La Mancha through whose voice and letters Cervantes will, from time to time, satirize social life in the small towns and villages there which he knew so well and did not much like. Not until the end of chapter 7 do Don Quixote and Sancho take the road again, the knight meanwhile having shown himself to be as crazed on the subject of knight errantry as he ever was. His plan, suggested to him by Sansón not without ulterior motive, is to travel to Saragossa to participate in the annual jousting which took place in the Aragonese capital on St George's day. But first he is determined to go to Toboso to pay his respects to Dulcinea (whom he has still never seen) and to obtain her permission to make the journey.

Sancho is alarmed. In Part I he had lyingly claimed that he had been to Toboso, had seen Dulcinea on Don Quixote's behalf and brought back a message from her. The consequences of his lies have now caught up with him; Don Quixote naturally supposes that Sancho can conduct him without difficulty to Dulcinea's 'palace' in Toboso since he has been there before. One of the most memorable comic scenes in the book then follows. Sancho tries admitting that he had never actually seen Dulcinea but the knight simply treats this confession as a joke in bad taste and will have none of it. Sancho is eventually forced to have recourse to Don Quixote's favourite explanation that enchanters have changed the natural appearance of reality: the travellers encounter outside Toboso three peasant girls mounted on donkeys; Sancho selects the most unprepossessing of the three to be Dulcinea, tells his master about the rich finery in which she is supposedly dressed and the splendid horses on which she and her 'retainers' are mounted and, kneeling before her on the road, addresses her as Dulcinea in the mock grandiloquent tones he has heard his master use. Don Quixote, however, is not always so ready with his hallucinations as he was in Part I; he can only see three village girls on donkeys, not his princess and her ladies. Nevertheless, observing Sancho's deferential language and acts, he concludes that he must indeed at last be in Dulcinea's presence even if his enemies the enchanters have made her look like an ugly peasant girl. The encounter ends in farce. The girls think they are being mocked by a pair of wayside wags and swear at them before fleeing on their donkeys. Sancho hypocritically curses the ill-intentioned magicians for what they have done to his master's vision. The squire's growing sense of superiority over Don Quixote is much increased, at least for the time being, by the success of this deception. But he is not capable of drawing the obvious conclusions from the experience about the validity of Don Quixote's world of chivalry in general.

Various other adventures follow. In one of them Don Quixote encounters, not to his surprise, another knight errant camping nearby for the night with his squire. He is, however, taken aback when the new arrival informs him that the proudest achievement of his career was when he met the famous Don Quixote in battle, defeated him, and forced him to confess that Dulcinea was inferior to his own patroness, Casilda de Vandalia. Since knights cannot lie and must treat each other with courtesy, the real Don Quixote responds to this information by once more seeing the hand of his enemies the enchanters at work: they have obviously let a false Quixote loose on the world. The two knights eventually fight over the respective merits of their ladies. Because of a miscalculation on the part of his foe, Don Quixote unexpectedly wins. It is then discovered, in the daylight, that his enemy has the appearance of none other than Sansón Carrasco while his squire, who has been wearing a large false nose to emphasize the burlesque nature of the encounter, looks like a man from their village whom Don Quixote and Sancho both know. The kindly Sansón had thought he might contrive to get Don Quixote back home and also have some fun by disguising himself as a rival knight errant. The plan was that he would defeat the mad knight in battle and then order him, as the laws of chivalry allowed the victor to do, to return to his village. But nothing turns out as planned; the bogus knight's project, apart from his own humiliation, has only resulted in convincing Don Quixote that he has notched up a famous victory as a knight errant; the little problem of his defeated opponent's apparent resemblance to his friend Sansón Carrasco is easily disposed of as yet another enchanter's trick.

Shortly afterwards the pair meet on the road a well-dressed man in a green topcoat who lives not far off. Cervantes's insistence on the colour of the gentleman's coat is ironical: green, symbol of youthful vigour, turns out to fit Don Quixote's new acquaintance very badly. The Knight in the Green Topcoat—named Don Diego de Miranda—seems, at first sight, to be a sort of ideal Christian country gentleman, well-off but living modestly with his family, a model of prudence, literate but careful to read only religious books or works of entertainment that represent no threat to morality (romances of chivalry had never, he explained, been seen in his house). He goes in for some mild hunting, but not of big or dangerous game. He tells Don Quixote that he never gossips or listens to gossip, that he is regular in his religious devotions and constantly gives to charity. This worthy figure is presented by Cervantes with some irony, as when Sancho kneels before him believing him to be a living saint. Not knowing anything about chivalric romance, the new acquaintance speedily concludes that he has met an incomprehensible madman. However he is less certain about this conclusion when the latter treats him to a sententious but well-informed and well-argued discourse on poetry and the poet's task. He soon reverts to his first opinion, however, when the travellers come up with two carts each containing a caged lion being sent from North Africa as a present for the king. Don Quixote determines that here is his chance, like other heroes in the romances, to kill a fierce animal in single combat. He forces the carter to open one of the cages and, despite the entreaties of carter, Sancho, and the gentleman in the green topcoat, advances sword in hand on the lion in the open cage. The lion, however, fails to oblige. It takes a leisurely look at Don Quixote and then, without leaving the open cage, turns round and settles down, exposing its hind quarters contemptuously to the knight. Instead of angrily provoking the animal to attack, Don Quixote, his ardour having cooled, rather readily allows himself to be convinced that he has sufficiently demonstrated the valour expected of him. It is one of several occasions in Part II when he not only seems to lack the irascible *élan* that drove him in Part I, but leaves the reader with the impression that he acts as he does more because he feels it is expected of him than because he wants to. The stay in Don Diego's house which follows leaves Don Diego and his pedantic student son bewildered by the good sense that is mixed up with their guest's madness. Don Diego has sometimes been thought to represent Cervantes's ideal of a reasonable, middle-of-the-road Christian country gentleman, but any close reading of the text makes it clear that the veteran of Lepanto viewed with a satirical eye his host's unadventurous and self-satisfied domesticity.

Chapters 19–22 are devoted to a pastoral tale, 'Camacho's Wedding'. This is, like those in Part I, dependent on improbable occurrences and unlikely, though morally uplifting, human responses to them. The story centres on the lavish village wedding festivities arranged for his marriage by the rich farmer bridegroom, Camacho. It tells how, by faking his own public suicide, Camacho's unwilling bride's own preferred choice for a husband, Basilio, was able to marry her under Camacho's nose. Don Quixote, declaring that, in love as in war, stratagems and deceits are legitimate, surprisingly approves what has happened. This story is not an autonomous interpolation; it develops as part of the experiences of the two travellers, and both knight and squire play parts in it.

Chapters 22–3 contain the adventure which, to judge by the number of subsequent references to it, Cervantes wanted his readers to regard as the most important of all those recounted in Part II. Its underlying theme represents a new approach to the problem of the relationship between truth and appearance. The adventure is concerned with Don Quixote's lone descent into the Cave of Montesinos and his account, when he is hauled out of it, of the marvellous things he has seen and experienced down there. The name of the cave shows that it then had associations in local folklore with a mythical French hero of

Charlemagne's time, Montesinos, who is the subject of one
or two well-known Spanish ballads. Cervantes for this
adventure uses a rich blend of folkloric, ballad, and
romance themes to create a little masterpiece of enigmatic
parody and burlesque at the expense both of Don Quixote
and of the ballad interpretations of medieval history. The
hero's trial by ordeal in the form of a visit to an underworld
inhabited by famous personages held in thrall by magic is
common enough in both literature and folklore.
Approximate models for Montesinos's cave can be found in
several Spanish chivalric romances as well as in Ariosto's
Orlando Furioso. The discovery in the cave of an
underworld of splendid palaces and of imposing tombs of
dead heroes who are allowed the momentary gift of speech
and prophecy is not unusual either. Cervantes elects to
centre his account mainly on the ballads about Montesinos.
Much of the fun is at the expense of the fact that, in the
ballads, Montesinos, after the defeat of the French at
Roncevaux, is supposed to have removed the heart of his
dead companion-in-arms, Durandarte, and taken it back to
France to hand it over to the latter's chosen lady, Belerma.
Cervantes's chief burlesque tool here is, through Don
Quixote's words, to treat this popular legend as if it were
true history and submit it to a wealth of invented 'realistic'
descriptive detail and pedantic explanation which the
knight believes will add conviction to his tale but which in
fact anchors it firmly in the shallows of burlesque epic.

The knight, when he is hauled up from the cave, is found
to be in a trance. When he wakes up he begins his account
of what he had seen there. The question is: does he really
believe he has seen what he describes, or has he invented
the whole thing consciously, claiming to have had, while
underground, an experience which he wished he could have
had? In the latter case we would have to conclude that Don
Quixote's confidence in the reality of his chivalric world
was now flagging and required this kind of artificial boost.
Cide Hamete (i.e. Cervantes) refuses to express an opinion

as to whether the story is true or false. Sancho is, however, in no doubt that his master is lying for, among other things, the knight claims that he had seen in the cave his beloved Dulcinea and her two attendants, still in their enchanted form as peasant girls, cavorting like goats. He expects this point to convince Sancho of the truth of his story. However, since in this case Sancho himself was the 'enchanter' he merely laughs at what he regards as final proof of Don Quixote's untruthfulness. As if to make sure that the reader is in no way encouraged to treat this affair other than as a burlesque parody carried out at his own expense by Don Quixote himself, Cervantes has him claim, in a further attempt to establish his veracity by bringing in factual detail, that Dulcinea was so hard-up in her enchanted captivity that she asked him to lend her his small change.

Taking it all in all, it is hard to believe that Cervantes himself wrote the Cave of Montesinos episode with any other conscious intention than that of ringing some highly original changes on the comic theme which dominates the book. It would take the revolutionary alteration in the traditional relationship between Don Quixote and his readers brought by Romanticism to change, by interpreting them symbolically, that way of perceiving the meaning of these chapters.

Balladry is also the source of the next important occurrence in the knight's career. One evening, while staying at a wayside inn, he and Sancho attend a puppet-show given there by an itinerant puppeteer. Its subject is an old ballad describing the rescue from the Moors in Saragossa, in Charlemagne's time, of a captive Christian lady, Melisendra, by her husband, Gaiferos. Cervantes, mainly through the verbal description of events in the puppet theatre by the puppeteer's naïve and over-eager boy assistant, contrives another amusing send-up of popular ballad history. Don Quixote, predictably, gets carried away by the spectacle of even puppet Moorish knights in battle with Christians and attacks them with his sword, smashing

63

up the puppet theatre in the process. Once again his lunatic hallucinations in the name of chivalric ideals have harmed others and made him ridiculous. Before the performance, Don Quixote and Sancho had been much surprised by the familiarity the puppeteer's supposedly talking monkey showed with them and their doings. It turns out that the puppeteer is none other than Ginés de Pasamonte, the most intelligent but also most villainous of the prisoners released by the knight in Part I.22.

In chapter 30, having crossed the River Ebro on his way to Saragossa, Don Quixote first meets the unnamed Duke and Duchess whose invitation to stay he enthusiastically accepts and in whose splendid country palace and park most of the action will now take place, until chapter 58. It is impossible to follow in any detail in this summary the many closely described burlesque events and comic conversations that now follow crowded together, so I shall confine myself to some general remarks about what happens in these chapters.

The Duke and Duchess are both enthusiastic readers of chivalric romance and have also enjoyed Part I of *Don Quixote*. They recognize the knight and his squire with delight as characters from that book when they meet them and resolve to have fun, particularly at Don Quixote's expense, 'treating him as a knight errant during the days he remained with them and arranging all the ceremonies usually found in the books of chivalry'. This they do. The staff of the palace and all the material resources available there are mobilized to stage a series of complicated burlesque pageants and other happenings based on material from the romances or on events in Part I, particularly those which concern Dulcinea. The knight is completely duped and Sancho, who has been turning increasingly sceptical about the whole situation in which he has become involved, is once more convinced, by what he sees and hears, that the world of chivalry is a real one.

The Duke and Duchess are remarkably unfeeling

aristocratic pranksters; some of their jokes involve causing physical harm to their two guests. Among the hoaxes they set up is one when they arrange for the figure of Merlin to appear and to inform Don Quixote that the disenchantment of Dulcinea can only be brought about if Sancho administers 3,300 strokes to his own bare buttocks—a joke that carries on being referred to with somewhat tiresome repetitiveness until the very end of the book. Don Quixote is portrayed as firmly believing in 'Merlin's' promise, which places Dulcinea and her disenchantment in a context of low burlesque. Even Don Quixote's possible sexual desires and apprehensions are made fun of by facing him with faked temptations to be disloyal to his Platonic love for Dulcinea. Sometimes the japes go wrong, as when one of the Duchess's dimmer ladies-in-waiting believes that Don Quixote really is a knight errant and genuinely seeks his help in that capacity, to the annoyance of her mistress; or when the Duke's resident priestly 'director of conscience', indignant at the indecorous presence at the Duke's table of a madman and a talkative and foolish peasant, rebukes the Duke for entertaining such guests and denounces Don Quixote to his face for being so mad as to believe in the truth of chivalric romance. This episode points up the boldness of Cervantes in portraying two members of the highest nobility in the land consorting in their palace on close terms with a peasant and an insane gentleman. Cervantes does not fail to exploit, either, the opportunities the whole situation offers for once more probing the weathercock mutability of prose fiction in the making; the Duke and Duchess sometimes get things wrong because, while they know the Don Quixote of Part I, they are not acquainted with what has previously happened to him in Part II, to which they themselves now belong. They have to learn about Part II's events from their visitors themselves. The Duchess then disconcerts Sancho by playing on her superior position to put it to him that perhaps it was he, not Don Quixote, who saw Dulcinea transformed by an enchanter when he supposed her to be a peasant girl; maybe she really was the beautiful lady the knight believed her to be.

The chapters involving the Duke and Duchess represent the final apotheosis of Sancho Panza. He frequently holds the floor conversationally; he has long discussions with the Duchess who, on one occasion, remarks that she thinks him madder but also more amusing than his master. The Duke has promised Sancho that he will secure him the governorship of the island on which he has set his heart since the beginning of Part I, and duly sends him off as its 'governor' to a place on his estates which Sancho is assured is an island called Barataria. An elaborate series of tricks and hoaxes at Sancho's expense have been arranged there and he has an extremely uncomfortable time, but the whole project backfires somewhat when it is discovered that, in many ways, Sancho deals with unexpected discretion with the pseudo-problems set up to test him as governor. Sancho, however, soon concludes that his ambition to become a person of power and wealth was a foolish one; he voluntarily abandons his 'island' to resume his role as Don Quixote's squire. However he never understands that he is the victim of a practical joke and, since the whole experience was a burlesque fake and gave him no genuine insights, either on a personal or public level, into what it was like to be a ruler, we are left to ponder the question whether salutary disillusion reached by such methods is or is not valid. Social satire directed at various levels of society is more prominent in these chapters than anywhere else in the book.

We do not know how Cervantes had up to now intended to proceed in the rest of Part II, except that he was committed to get Don Quixote to the city of Saragossa for the tournament there. He was probably still proceeding with that intention when he set about writing chapter 59. At this point, however, a catastrophe occurred in real life whose repercussions drastically affected the rest of the book. This was the appearance, in the autumn of 1614, of Avellaneda's Second Part. The bogus Second Part is a work which reflects the dislike of the literary establishment for

Cervantes while, paradoxically, by its very existence, paying tribute to the literary fame of his creation.

This is not the place to attempt an evaluation of Avellaneda's book except to note that it deviates markedly in plot from its model. It often shows us Don Quixote and Sancho in urban situations. Dulcinea has been abandoned from the beginning by Avellaneda's knight, whom his new biographer incarcerates in several prisons and, finally, in a lunatic asylum in Toledo. Avellaneda, a pious and establishment-minded writer, turned Don Quixote into a mere demented, unlikeable figure of fun and Sancho into the sort of unredeemed rustic clown which literature traditionally expected peasants to be.

Cervantes did not allow his anger to close his mind to the fact that the unexpected arrival of a 'genuine' pseudo-*Don Quixote* in the hands of readers could be used by him artistically in a positive way: to give yet another new dimension to his exploration of the tricks that could be played with fictional reality. In chapter 59, while Don Quixote and Sancho are eating their supper in an inn, they hear the two fellow-guests next door discussing in adverse terms what they refer to as the 'second part' of *Don Quixote*, which they are reading. They specially criticize the fact that in it the knight is portrayed as no longer in love with Dulcinea. This is too much for the listening Don Quixote who shouts out that Dulcinea is still his only love and that he will use his sword on anyone who says otherwise. The existence of Avellaneda's book is then revealed to him. Confronted 'in the flesh', as it were, by the genuine knight and squire, the two gentlemen concerned agree that the work they have been reading is all lies. When the knight further learns that in Avellaneda's book his long-awaited arrival in Saragossa is described, he announces that he will not now continue his journey there but instead will go to Barcelona, thus, he explains, conclusively proving that his unauthorized biographer is a liar! But is Don Quixote correct when he supposes that a switch of his destination from Saragossa to Barcelona will prove Avellaneda's version of events to be a lie? It is a difficult question in the context of fiction. The reader knows very well that, when Avellaneda wrote his version, Saragossa really was, on the authority of the book's real author, the knight's destination. In chapter 72 Cervantes carries out a spectacular *coup* against his unknown enemy by kidnapping a prominent character from Avellaneda's book, Don Alvaro Tarfe. Don Alvaro, discovering that the 'real' Don Quixote and Sancho are quite unlike their homonyms whom he had had dealings with in the other work, signs an affidavit to the effect that the latter were impostors.

After chapter 59 Cervantes, now in a hurry to get Part II to press before the rival volume became too well established in the reading public's mind, appears at times to have lost his way. Improbabilities tend to pile up and both Don Quixote and Sancho are, in some of these chapters, overshadowed by external events. Curiously enough Cervantes seems to have become a bit confused between what had been written about the knight and the squire by Avellaneda, whose work he had of course just carefully read, and what he himself had written long ago in Part I or even more recently in Part II.

Once he is in Catalonia, Don Quixote falls in with a powerful bandit leader, Roque Guinart, with whom he becomes friends and under whose protection he even places himself for a while. For the first time a contemporary and well-known historical figure is identified and turned into a functioning character in the book. It is noticeable that Cervantes treats the Catalan outlaw in that unexpectedly sympathetic way in which, in his *Exemplary Novels*, he sometimes presents other professional criminals; but here such an approach is at odds with the decorum of his own tale.

Chapters 61–5 take place in Barcelona, where the knight is the guest of a rich and well-connected gentleman, Don Antonio Moreno, who, like the Duke and Duchess, proposes to have fun at Don Quixote's expense. Though, we are told, Don Antonio does not intend his jokes to be hurtful, the knight is, in fact, exposed in Barcelona to ridicule, public and private. An elaborate episode is that of Don Quixote's formal visit as an honoured guest to the squadron of royal galleys stationed in the port. He is received with full naval honours by the commander of the galleys and hobnobs with the viceroy. He and Sancho even put to sea aboard one of the galleys when these go into action against a Turkish brigantine off the coast. Cervantes once again uses the occasion to draw on his memories of his own naval experiences. The whole affair is mixed up with a further instalment of the story of the search of a Morisco exile, Ricote, for his lost daughter. Ricote, a former inhabitant of Don Quixote's native village and an old friend of Sancho, had made his first appearance, disguised as a pilgrim, in chapter 54. The missing girl, improbably, appears here disguised as a male Turk, who, as commander of the captured brigantine, bravely awaits execution by being hanged from the Spanish galley's yard-arm. Her Christian Spanish lover, the company learn from her, is hiding in Algiers dressed as a woman to avoid the unwelcome sexual attention his handsome appearance would attract from male Turks if they knew his gender. This is plainly one of those stories meant to astonish the reader on which Cervantes, like his contemporaries, enjoyed exercising his powers of invention. Of course, in the end, everything is happily resolved; the beauty, true love and, despite appearances, the Christian steadfastness of Ricote's daughter triumph. Cervantes's introduction here of an actual Spanish political problem (the recent expulsion of the Moriscos, about which he contrives to take up a covertly ambiguous position) places the final chapters of *Don Quixote* squarely in the Spain of the early seventeenth century. Some of these episodes strain the reader's credulity too far; they remind us more of those to be found in Cervantes's romance *Persiles and Sigismunda*, on which, of course, he was also at work at this time.

The reception aboard the fleet and subsequent naval action represent, it must be noted, the knight's first and only encounter with real war and its instruments. He does not emerge with any credit from it. Cut off from the literary guidance of the chivalric romances which have always told him how to conduct himself, he is frightened by some of the shipboard routines; Sancho, too, is roughly handled by the galley slaves. Like the chapters in the ducal palace, these Barcelona chapters are a stumbling-block to any critic wishing to believe that Cervantes, in Part II, is less interested than he had been in Part I in depicting Don Quixote and Sancho as figures of fun.

After this diversion the narrative describes the episode which is really to mark the beginning of the end for Don Quixote. One day on the beach at Barcelona, where the knight is exercising himself fully armed on Rocinante, he is challenged by another similarly armed knight who might also have stepped from a romance of chivalry (II. 64). The stranger calls himself the Knight of the White Moon. He challenges Don Quixote, calling on him, if defeated, to admit that the challenger's own lady, 'whoever she may be', is incomparably more beautiful than Dulcinea, and to agree to go home and to abstain from knight errantry for a year. This is a return to a world the mad knight understands. The reader's awareness that we are in a new burlesque and parodic situation is assured because the Knight of the White Moon when addressing Don Quixote uses the discourteous second person singular, a gross breach of manners which the latter does not seem to notice.

The ensuing single combat takes place in the presence of the viceroy and a distinguished company, again with a loss of probability that recalls this time Avellaneda rather than the delicate touch of Cervantes. Don Quixote is rapidly defeated. Lying on the ground in the power of the victor he declares that he prefers death to any renunciation of his belief that Dulcinea is the most beautiful woman in the world. The kindly victor forgoes this condition. However, bound by the logic of his own insanity, Don Quixote does accept the second condition and, with it, the suspension for a year of his activities as a knight errant. Symbolically he re-enters the city no longer mounted on Rocinante but in a sedan chair. The Knight of the White Moon is, of course, Sansón Carrasco making his second attempt to rescue Don Quixote from his infirmity. The success of Sansón's ruse does not earn him any applause from the gentlemen of Barcelona; Don Antonio Moreno chides him for spoiling the amusement of the whole world by wanting to cure the insanity of the most diverting madman to be found in it.

The remaining chapters recount the journey of knight and squire back to their village. A further stay with the Duke and Duchess, and one more elaborate burlesque arranged by them at the expense of knight and squire, pads things out with comedy or farce as do some other humiliating experiences suffered by the knight, who still keeps on harrying Sancho to flagellate himself in order to secure the disenchantment of Dulcinea. Don Quixote now seriously thinks of adopting the role of a personality from pastoral literature. This possibility will remain in his mind until the end of his madness. When the pair reach their village he is put to bed gravely ill. After a long sleep he wakes up apparently now sane, declares that his name is Alonso Quijano, denounces the absurdities of chivalric romance, recognizes that he has been out of his mind (though he has a surprisingly full memory of what he did when mad) and then dies amid the lamentation of his friends after asking Sancho's pardon for having caused the latter to appear to be as mad as himself. Cervantes is, however, careful not to abandon the burlesque tone when he (or rather, Cide Hamete) describes Don Quixote's death and burial. Any other potential continuers of the story are warned off by the firm assertion that the knight (likened, in his epitaph, we are told, to a scarecrow) 'lies well and truly stretched out' in his grave, incapable of ever making a third sally.

In modern times critics have often attempted comparative evaluations of the two parts of *Don Quixote*. The contradictory results obtained suggest that the critics' subjective preferences play a large part in such an exercise. Moreover the propriety of separating for this purpose two parts of the same story written by the same author is less certain than it might seem to be at first sight. After 1617, readers both Spanish and foreign have been accustomed to encountering the complete history of Don Quixote within the same covers. Until our own time critics have rarely, if ever, considered the two parts separately. Important differences do, as we have seen, exist between the two parts but it can hardly be said that any of these changes are not potentially present in Part I. The so-called 'Sanchification' of Don Quixote and 'Quixotification' of Sancho offer an example of this. The many continuities between Part I and Part II need to be stressed as well as the differences.

6 The madness of Don Quixote

To sum up: he buried himself in these books [of chivalry] to such an extent that he spent his nights, from sundown to sunrise, reading them as if it were bright daylight and his days, from daybreak to sunset, blear-eyed as if it were night. So it came about that, from lack of sleep and too much reading, his brain became dry and he eventually lost his sanity. (*Don Quixote* I.1)

Don Diego asked his son what sense he had made of their guest's wits. He replied: 'All the best doctors and all the best fair-copyists there are in the world will not be able to correct the flawed scrawl of his madness: he is a particoloured lunatic, full of lucid intervals.' (*Don Quixote* II.18)

Don Quixote's madness is the pivot on which Cervantes's entire book turns. It makes possible the parody of chivalric romances that he set out to write. It sets up the confrontation between appearance and reality which is the theme that underlies the parody. Above all, for Cervantes and for generations of readers of *Don Quixote* after him until the nineteenth century, the madness of the knight was the quality that made him, and the book, a comic one. Small wonder then that, both by means of direct authorial comment and through the comments of many of the characters who meet Don Quixote, Cervantes constantly reminds his readers that we are witnessing the ridiculous antics of or listening to the utterances of a madman.

What kind of a madness is it that Don Quixote suffers from? We know that it has been brought on by his frenetic reading of chivalric romance, but that the condition itself appears permanent. In modern times *Quixote* critics show a marked desire to present the knight as a character who, apart from the unhinging effect on him of the chivalry books, was otherwise an entirely sane individual. The evidence of the text is, however, wholly against such an interpretation. Using contemporary medical beliefs about the psychological effects of the dominant 'humours' on the mind, Cervantes from the start is careful to point out that Don Quixote's brain has dried out. This abnormal condition of his brain is reflected in his physical appearance. Thus, at the beginning of Part II, and as a sign that he is still mad, we are told that his flesh was now so dried-up-looking that he resembled a mummy (II.1). To add to the impression of sickness his complexion, too, is yellowish. His thinness and his lantern-jawed appearance also point to a serious abnormality affecting his whole being. What makes Don Quixote's madness 'never before seen', as Cervantes insists, is that it takes the form of believing that the fictions of chivalric romance are not only historically true but that he himself can expect to find them re-enacted, or re-enactable, in the contemporary world, a process which leads him to the ultimate insanity of believing that he has converted himself into one of these figures from fiction.

One of the apparent ambiguities about Don Quixote's madness concerns the 'lucid intervals' during which he behaves, and, particularly, speaks with apparent prudence and good sense. In terms of the medical beliefs of the age, 'lucid intervals' were a normal feature of insanity. A Spanish dictionary of Cervantes's time describes the condition as madness characterized by remissions. The seventeenth-century English essayist Samuel Butler, himself a student of *Don Quixote*, comments on this aspect of madness more than once. He makes the point, with reference to the way Cervantes treats his knight, that, though the latter, in his lucid intervals, *seems* much wiser than a natural fool like Sancho, in fact Sancho is really the wiser of the pair. This is because Sancho's foolishness is part of the natural order of things, given his peasant status, whereas everything that Don Quixote does is a facet of the deviation from that natural order which madness necessarily is. Cervantes, who was undoubtedly interested in clinical madness, certainly shared the contemporary view of a madman's lucid intervals. We recall his story of the experienced warden of the asylum for the insane in Seville who was unconvinced that one of his charges was cured despite the extreme good sense and prudence of his behaviour and discourse over an extended period. The warden was eventually forced by others to agree to the 'cured' patient's release but, as he was about to leave the asylum, the latter, under stress, gave himself away by declaring himself to be the god Neptune (II.1). The point of this story is that it was related by the Barber to Don Quixote with malicious intent to see how he responded to a case similar to his own.

Cervantes plays up Don Quixote's lucid intervals for all he is worth. Their existence appealed to his sense of paradox and his belief that it was a function of art to surprise. They also opened up opportunities for wide-ranging discourses and discussions in which the knight could participate, often taking the lead, without doing violence to probability, thus vastly extending the narrative and intellectual reach of the book beyond what a strict adherence to portraying Don Quixote in his lunatic moments would have permitted. Nevertheless Cervantes is usually careful, by some trick of language, style, or situation, to remind us that, even in his lucid moments, we have to do with a comical madman. Sometimes Cervantes achieves his purpose of pulling the rug from under Don Quixote's lucidity by merely recording an inept or ironical comment on his utterances by Sancho or another bystander, or by making the knight himself use a vulgar or otherwise inappropriate expression much below the stylistic level he is striving to maintain. The lucid moments of Don Quixote are thus enveloped in ambiguity, not just at the expense of the knight himself but also at the expense of the reader. What exactly, the reader is invited to ask himself, is the status of what seems on one level to be sound sense when it emerges from the mouth of a person we know to be deranged? One other view about mental illness in Cervantes's time was that madness could produce manifestations of intellectual brilliance in a person who, when sane, had shown no signs of it; Cervantes uses that belief as the basis for his short story about another madman, 'The Glass Licenciate' ('El licenciado vidriera'). The latter, when his reason returns, loses all his intellectual brilliance and reverts to being a person of no particular interest. We are not given time to assess Don Quixote's intellectual status when he is cured but those who meet him recognize that in his case too his madness and his importance are inseparable: Don Antonio Moreno, it will be recalled, complains to Sansón Carrasco in Barcelona:

> God forgive you for the offence you have committed against the whole world by wanting to make sane the most amusing madman to be found in it! Do you not understand, sir, that any benefit which a sane Don Quixote may bring can never equal the pleasure that he gives with his mad absurdities?

There are other aspects of Don Quixote which show that Cervantes wished to offer his readers a finely observed portrait of a comical madman. There is the topsy-turvy logic with which he can always defend his hallucinatory world against the challenge of reality, usually by appealing to the authority of the romances or by explaining that he is the victim of the machinations of hostile enchanters. It is the kind of defence familiar to those who try to treat cases of hallucination. A great deal of the comedy depends, of course, on the fact that, confronted by an insane person, the sane often find it easier to pretend to go along with his fantasies than to risk trouble by disputing them. In *Don*

Quixote, however—most prominently during the stay in the palace of the Duke and Duchess but also on various other occasions—people go beyond merely pretending to accept the hallucinations as true; they deliberately, for their own amusement, fabricate situations which are intended to cause the knight to display his insanity and in which they themselves pretend to believe. This capacity of Don Quixote to 'contaminate' sane people, driving them to behave as if they too were crazed is something remarked upon in the text. But while modern readers can see in all this disturbing hints of the blurred state of the boundary between sanity and insanity, there is no reason to think that Cervantes or his earlier readers doubted that, in real life, the borderline was perfectly clear. Cervantes, through Cide Hamete, suggests, it is true, that the Duke and Duchess are very near to appearing ridiculous themselves since they put such an effort into setting up machinery for laughing at two fools (II.70). But, when the question is faced head on, the Cervantine position is conventional enough. Tomé Cecial, Sansón Carrasco's bogus squire on the occasion of the episode of the Knight of the Mirrors, asks the bachelor: 'Who is more mad; he who is so because he cannot help it or he who chooses madness deliberately?' Sansón's reply is categorical: 'He who is mad without willing it will always remain so'; to be truly mad is not a matter of choice.

One further and important point arising from Don Quixote's status as a madman should be emphasized: he could have no legal or moral responsibility for his acts as long as he remained mad, a fact to which the text, in the name of verisimilitude, more than once draws attention. If he made too much of a social nuisance of himself (as he does in Avellaneda's *Quixote*) he would be locked away for safety's sake, but otherwise the law would leave him alone, even if he committed minor criminal offences (cf. the Priest's remarks to the constables in I.46).

The figure of Sancho Panza is inseparable from that of

Don Quixote; neither can do without the other. Cervantes, in all his works, has a liking for grouping his characters in pairs; but the Don Quixote–Sancho relationship is of a different order of intimacy. Cervantes seems to have thought of knight and squire as representative incarnations of the twin aspects of folly—the folly of the madman and the folly of the simpleton. In Part I.30, Cardenio's Dorotea, her troubled love-life having been now put right, joins the plot of the Priest and the Barber to get Don Quixote home by setting up a fake chivalric situation. She pretends to be the Princess Micomicona, come from Black Africa to seek the knight's help against a usurping giant there. Don Quixote, of course, is readily taken in. So is Sancho, who sees the material benefits of being an African governor if he could persuade his master to forget about Dulcinea and marry the 'princess'; he himself, as such a governor, could also become a trader in slaves and make a lot of money. Moved by greed and ambition he kneels before the ex-Dorotea and seeks to kiss her hand in token of vassalage. The author intervenes in the narrative to ask: 'Who among the bystanders could not laugh, seeing the madness of the master and the folly of the servant?' As if to make sure the point is not missed, the same rhetorical question is put again five chapters later.

Sancho's character and his role in the book are, perhaps surprisingly, more complex than those of Don Quixote. His very name implies a contradiction: 'Sancho' in popular parlance was believed to be an appropriate Christian name for a man who was 'saintly, healthy and good'; 'Panza' (literally 'belly') was used to describe a traditional comic figure in student rags characterized by his huge stomach, short body and long legs. This same mixture of contradictory qualities is carried over into Sancho's character, which is partly based on the figure of the rustic simpleton who was a stock clown in the Spanish theatre as it was in Cervantes's younger days and in part incorporates characteristics of the sagacious and cunning peasant of folklore and popular oral tales. No doubt this second aspect of Sancho also owed a good deal to Cervantes's own extensive dealings with peasants during his days as a royal commissary. The satirical cameos of Sancho's wife, Teresa, and of her view of village life in La Mancha which appear in the exchanges of letters in Part II certainly reflect them. From the rustic fool of the theatre Sancho gets his stupid credulity, his greed, his cowardice and, probably, his rustic speech. This side of him is symbolized by his ass and his attachment to it. But contradicting it are the qualities he has derived from the peasant of folklore and from Cervantes's own experience of what peasants were really like: his astuteness, his ability to turn situations to his material advantage, his self-confidence, his inconsequential loquacity, his refusal to be intimidated by superior social rank, and his habit of turning to the wisdom of popular proverbs to comment on situations. The alternation of foolish credulity and astute scepticism in Sancho mirrors his master's alternation between insane hallucinations and 'lucid intervals'.

Sancho's original function was to provide Don Quixote with a companion to whom he could talk, thus allowing the author to exercise his natural genius as a writer of dialogue and to provide insights into both men's minds and motives through their own utterances. Sancho's role was subordinate but delicate. He had to be credulous, otherwise his role as squire could not be convincingly explained. But he also had to combine this with a considerable measure of good sense so that he could be relied on to take up a realistic, even antagonistic, attitude to his master's misinterpretations of circumstances, thus letting the reader know what the real situation was. But Sancho speedily starts to do more than merely gloss Don Quixote's doings and utterances for the reader's benefit. He goes wherever Don Quixote goes, sharing not only his meals and, when they are staying at an inn, his bedroom, but also taking part in conversations with those who are the knight's social equals or superiors.

Sancho is already very much on top in some chapters of Part I, specially after his pretended visit to Dulcinea has taught him that the credulity of his master is such that he will believe any lie as long as this fits in with his expectations. But the apotheosis of Sancho, of course, takes place in Part II, after he has learnt that he is the second most important personage in the published account of their adventures and that there are some readers who enjoy reading about him most of all. In Part II the narrator, apart from the chapters devoted to his fake governorship, often allows Sancho his head, openly observing that he is becoming less stupid and more intelligent—a comment which, ironically, is put in the mouth of Don Quixote and secures the courteous reply from the squire that the latter's conversation has acted like manure on the barren earth of his wits. No less ironically it is Don Quixote who, in the palace of the Duke and Duchess, supplies a eulogy of Sancho which undoubtedly sums up the qualities of the squire as, by then, his author, too, had come to see him:

> I wish Your Graces to understand that Sancho Panza is one of the most amusing squires who ever served any knight errant. At times the simplicities he utters are so to the point that wondering if he is being foolish or shrewd is a cause of no little pleasure. He performs knaveries enough to condemn him as a rogue and blunders enough to make of him a confirmed fool; he doubts everything yet believes everything; when I think he is about to fall headlong into some folly he comes out with wise remarks that, instead, raise him up to the heavens. (II.32)

The irony lies in the fact that the knight's description of Sancho as a wise fool also fits, with only minor alterations of wording, his own situation as a lunatic with intervals of apparent lucidity.

The madness of *Don Quixote* was to prove a stumbling-block for Romantic critics in their attempts to make a hero of him. They were liable to try to get over it simply by ignoring it or by pretending that it was something else. On the fact of the knight's madness the Cervantine text is, however, for once quite unambiguous. We should not overlook the originality and boldness of Cervantes's decision, at the beginning of the seventeenth century, to make the story of a comic madman the theme of a whole book. It was doubtless his awareness of this that caused him, mischievously using Don Quixote again as his spokesman, to make his one-off but famous defence of comedy and comic writing:

> To make jokes and to write wittily requires great genius: the most dextrous part in a play is that of the fool, for a man who wants to give the impression that he is a simpleton must not be one. (II.3)

The observation, as well as demanding proper recognition for comedy as a reputable literary form, reminds us by implication that, in Cervantes's time, madness was viewed as as much a legitimate cause of merriment as was natural folly.

7   Art entwined with laughter

Loud, heap miseries upon us yet entwine our arts with laughters low!
(James Joyce, *Finnegan's Wake*, 1939)

However, the Barber fixed things so that the goatherd forced Don
Quixote under him and rained down on him such a quantity of
punches to the face that the visage of the poor knight poured out as
much blood as did his own. The Canon and the Priest were bursting
with laughter; the constables jumped with joy; everyone cheered
them on as people do dogs tangled up in a fight. (*Don Quixote*, I.52)

Amiable reader, let the good Sancho go in peace, safe and sound, and
wait for the three bushels of laughter which will be yours when you
learn how he comported himself in his government. Meanwhile, get
ready to learn what happened to his master that night; if it does not
make you laugh, at least it will make you unfold your lips in an ape's
grin, for what happens to Don Quixote has to be applauded, maybe
with astonishment, maybe with laughter. (*Don Quixote*, II.44)

If Cervantes seems to leave us in no doubt that he thought
of Don Quixote as a madman and Sancho Panza as a
simpleton, though both were very unusual specimens of
their kind, we have also seen in previous chapters that he
is no less insistent that their doings and their sayings evoke
loud laughter from most bystanders. In particular when, as
frequently happens, the knight or the squire, or both
together, are in the process of getting physically injured,

mirth, not compassion, is the response aroused even in those who are their friends. The second passage quoted above is typical of many. Here we have two priests, one of them a close friend of Don Quixote, the other an important ecclesiastical dignitary, standing aside bursting with laughter at the spectacle of his wounding and humiliation; the Barber, another friend, has actually intervened to make sure Don Quixote is pinned in a position where the goatherd gets a proper chance to punch him in the face. Don Quixote's humiliation is compounded by the author, who subsequently intervenes to liken the bloody and unseemly fight between knight and goatherd to a scrimmage between two angry dogs. Yet we are obviously not intended to conclude from such a scene that Cervantes thought of the knight as the wronged victim of false or heartless friends. No such thing is hinted at and, on this and other occasions, no incompatibility between friendship and a readiness to laugh at and connive in a friend's misfortunes is suggested. The reason for this is not difficult to grasp as long as we remember the kind of book we are concerned with: Cervantes is writing a parody in the comic mode and all the characters must, to ensure comic decorum, contribute to the mirth-making. Beating up a figure of ridicule was an accepted convention of the mode.

Did Cervantes himself, as has sometimes been suggested, see that behind the fun his story perhaps presented situations and issues for which laughter was not the only possible response? The third of the passages heading this chapter is one of the very few occasions in the book when even a suspicion of support for such a conclusion can be located, in the apparent acceptance of astonishment as an alternative reader-reaction to laughter. But it must be doubted if Cervantes was even here doing more than indulge his penchant for antithetical utterance without regard for any profounder implications. The episode the passage introduces is one of sheer burlesque into which it is impossible to read anything likely to arouse in the reader the notion of fear associated with a simian grin: this is the occasion when one of the Duchess's maids, Altisidora, takes the lead in an elaborate charade in which she pretends to be tormented by love for Don Quixote and serenades him, supposedly in the hope of seducing him and so destroying the very keystone of his hallucinatory existence as a knight errant—his love for Dulcinea. Don Quixote is taken in; this evidence that young maidens evidently cannot resist his charms feeds his conviction that he is the equal of the handsome heroes of the romances or, indeed, is already numbered among them. But, of course, he resists the sham sexual blandishments offered by Altisidora, in a way which makes her, as well as him, look foolish. The episode ends, at least for the time being, when a sackful of frightened cats is let loose in his room and he is badly scratched. If Cervantes had had a passing thought, as he began to write this adventure, that the mockery and ill-treatment to which he submitted his knight was not necessarily always an occasion for laughter, he very soon banished it again.

Guffaws of laughter are not, of course, the only comic response the book sets out to arouse. Irony is continuously used with an accompanying conspiratorial wink to the reader, at the expense of both the knight and the squire and those who mock them. Good-humoured irony is all-pervasive in *Don Quixote*. It does not limit itself, traditionally, to saying the opposite of what is meant, or less than is meant. Cervantine irony often takes a more ambiguous route, seeming both to mean and perhaps not to mean what it appears to be saying. But the reader is normally left to detect and appreciate the irony unprompted. It is to make sure that the sound of raucous laughter which echoes through the book is not missed that Cervantes constantly intervenes.

Madness portrayed as a comical condition and laughter nearly always elbowing out compassion are the features of

Don Quixote that many modern readers find it difficult to accept. It is important to realize, however, that this kind of problem did not trouble readers during the first century and a half of the book's existence. In Spain itself, and in France and England, as many contemporary comments make plain, the work, except for the interpolated stories, was almost universally seen as wholly comical. The leading Spanish seventeenth-century literary historian categorized it (1670) as 'a most amusing creation whose hero is a new Amadis of Gaul fashioned out of ridicule'; long before that, Don Quixote and Sancho Panza had appeared as farcical characters on the stage and been incorporated into popular folk festivities in Spain as traditional comic figures. Accustomed as they were to parody used as a pretty crude literary genre, what seems to have impressed French readers and critics of the time was that Cervantes had given it in his book the epic scale and the originality and finesse to make a major literary form out of it. In England, too, it was as a supreme purveyor of the ridiculous that *Don Quixote* was long admired and imitated. Henry Fielding presented his own novel *Joseph Andrews* to his readers (1742) with an assurance that it was written in imitation of *Don Quixote*, so that he had made his characters 'people of inferior rank and manners' and, in consequence, the feelings and speech of the hero 'not sublime but ridiculous'. Tobias Smollett, himself one of several eighteenth-century English translators of the book, referred to Cervantes's book as 'an inimitable piece of ridicule' through which the author had converted romance into a much more useful and entertaining literary form by making it assume the garb of comedy concerned with the follies of everyday life.

Several French and English writers, though, also claimed that Cervantes's book had had social consequences. Père Rapin, writing in France in 1674, saw it as a brilliant satire on the Spanish nobility which it had rendered ridiculous. The same point was made by Richard Steele (c.1709). He complained that it had destroyed the spirit of gallantry in

Spain and that 'the humour of its ridicule' had done an injury to English high society too. Daniel Defoe claimed that he had heard that any Spanish noble now venturing to appear in public wearing the accoutrements of knighthood found himself the butt of the laughter of high and low alike who would point at him mockingly as a 'Don Quixote'.

In terms of attitudes that prevailed in contemporary Europe there is nothing surprising about the discovery that *Don Quixote* seemed to readers then a uniquely original funny book. Students of the nature of the ridiculous then believed that laughter was caused by any form of the 'ugly', that is by any kind of deviation from the natural order of things as we expect them to be; madness was clearly such a deviation. The distorting mask worn routinely by actors in ancient comedy was referred to frequently as symbolizing this connection between ugliness and the ridiculous. Writers of the time who sought to distinguish between tragedy and comedy found a distinction in terms of audience response. One of them, Alonso López Pinciano, explained that, in the case of tragedy, the audience felt itself involved in the emotional experiences going on on-stage. In the case of comedy an audience felt no such involvement; 'Although the actors experience distress and discontent,' he wrote, 'these, as I have said, do not pass across to the audience: on the contrary, the perturbation of the actor causes the audience to collapse with laughter.' This seems like an all-important key to any understanding of the way Cervantes conceived his book and the way he expected readers to respond to it. Of course, when, later on, they began to wish to identify with Don Quixote (or with Sancho Panza) the original pact made between writer and reader would necessarily break down.

Cervantes did not merely claim literary merit for his book. He also claimed, in the Prologue to Part I, a therapeutic effect for it; it would, as we have seen, make the sufferer from the disease of melancholia laugh. Contemporary medical theory held that the physiological consequences of the act of laughing did, indeed, have curative potential in respect of this and other diseases or morbid nervous states; the great seventeenth-century French writer Saint-Évremond meant to be taken literally when he assured an exiled friend in 1674 that, if he read *Don Quixote*, his unhappiness would be turned imperceptibly into feelings of joy.

The most convincing example of how the book is firmly anchored in the comic mode is provided by the way Cervantes presents the theme which dominates it: the relationship between appearance and reality. A modern Spanish critic has written: 'If there is in Cervantes one overall preoccupation, greater than all the rest, it is "What is the nature of objective reality?" ' This statement, as far as *Don Quixote* is concerned, is both true and at the same time deeply liable to mislead. It is true because the nature of the knight's hallucinatory view of the world, with the accompanying tendency of his hallucinations to get accepted by others for convenience's sake, or for comic purposes, creates confusion about what is true and what is false. But, as we have seen, the Spanish critic's comment is profoundly misleading if it suggests that the reader will find, in *Don Quixote*, any evidence that Cervantes was concerned on a serious level with the problem of the relationship between appearance and reality. His treatment of the theme is that of a conjurer who sees in it material out of which he can set up merry literary games to further his parody of the chivalric romances. Doubtless the games on this particular theme are capable of giving serious students of the basic philosophical problem that they make a jest of something to think about, but Cervantes issues no invitation to anyone to do that.

The impression that art is inextricably entwined with laughter in *Don Quixote* is amply confirmed by a study of the language in which the book is written; a preoccupation with securing a comic effect through language and style is constant in it except in the interpolated stories. Cervantes's views on language deserve closer scrutiny than they sometimes get. It is true that he repeatedly pronounces in favour of the early Renaissance doctrine that clarity and straightforwardness are the first requisites of good style. We recall the advice of the imaginary 'friend' in the Prologue to Part I:

> Endeavour to make your diction and sentences come out plain, harmonious and festive, using expressive, decorous and well-ordered words, painting your intention as best you can manage to do within the limits of the possible, setting out your thoughts without complicating them or making them obscure.

Many would-be translators of *Don Quixote*, wrestling with the impossible problem of finding adequate renderings for the puns and other forms of word-play in which Cervantes so frequently indulges in this book, must have wondered whether the 'friend's' admonitions were not meant to contain an element of irony. However, Cervantes's view of what constituted a plain and unadorned style has to be understood in the context of what Spanish was like in his day. Foreigners often commented then on Spaniards' addiction to metaphor in their speech, their liking for finding witty ways of saying things, their habit of using rhetorical questions and exclamatory utterances and their special fondness for larding their speech with popular proverbs and sententious aphorisms. 'Plain speech' for Cervantes, then, admitted all these characteristics. Moreover he is anything but a writer content, in his prose, to use conventional language as he found it; an outstanding merit of the style of *Don Quixote*, whether in narrative and descriptive passages or in the conversational ones, is the author's ability, at the right moment, to substitute for the expected word or phrase an unexpected one that vitalizes and dramatizes the statement, usually to achieve an ironic or straightforwardly ridiculous effect. A characteristic example of a technique employed to achieve what eighteenth-century English critics thought of as 'high burlesque' in the book occurs in Part I. 50, where Don Quixote is imagining a typical scene from a chivalric romance, as he often does. On this occasion he tells at length how a knight in full armour plunges unhesitatingly through a lake of burning pitch to emerge beneath it into a pastoral Elysium, where he is received into a magnificent palace and waited on by mysteriously silent maidens who serve him with a splendid repast. Thus far Don Quixote has largely maintained a properly elevated tone without faltering but now, when he reaches a key point in his tale and is about to describe the entry of a beautiful lady into the hall as his imaginary knight is sitting in his chair after the repast, Cervantes finally pricks the balloon of Don Quixote's fantasy by making him assert, with comical impropriety, that the knight at this crucial moment was 'perhaps picking his teeth as the custom is'. Unaware, as always, that he has slipped on a banana skin dropped by himself, he moves from burlesque into unconscious irony when he asks his listeners if his narrative does not convince them that any story of knight errantry is guaranteed to cause astonishment.

Another characteristic example of the way Cervantes uses unexpected language to secure burlesque effects is to be found near the end of Part I, when Sancho, believing his master to have been cudgelled to death, attempts a funeral oration over the 'body' in the tradition of the elegiac eulogies from the romances he has heard from the lips of Don Quixote himself (I.52). Unable to handle a task for which he is singularly ill-equipped, Sancho manages not only to trivialize his burlesque eulogy but also to turn it, in part, into condemnation, not praise, of his master:

Oh, you who were more generous than all the Alexanders, since for only eight months' service you have given me the best isle that the sea girds and surrounds! Oh, you who were humble before the haughty and haughty towards the humble, defier of dangers, tolerator of affronts, enamoured without cause, imitator of the virtuous, scourge of the wicked, enemy of knaves: in short, a knight errant, which is to say all that needs to be said.

Another feature of Cervantes's style in *Don Quixote* is his habit of using a cliché and then proceeding to gloss it or reinforce it in an exaggerated or otherwise absurd manner. A simple example of this technique occurs when, having explained that Don Quixote took up his position at the foot of an elm and Sancho at the foot of a beech, the narrator immediately comments: 'for the said trees and others like them have feet but no hands' (II.28), so extracting a kind of surrealist image of trees as armless humans by bringing into association two possible meanings of the word 'foot'. Another stylistic trick much to the fore in *Don Quixote* involves introducing a comparison which caricatures by gross exaggeration. An example of this occurs when a man recognizes his stolen packsaddle: 'Gentlemen, this saddle is as much mine as is the death I owe God and I know it is mine just as if I had given birth to it' (I.44). Despite his declared insistence on clarity of expression, Cervantes sometimes gives his readers something to puzzle over because of his recourse, even in his non-conversational prose, to the sort of sudden and logically unjustified jumping from one subject to another that is characteristic of ordinary speech—a device usually designed to permit a piece of word-play.

Perhaps, though, the most significant feature of Cervantes's use of language in *Don Quixote* is his fondness for combining antithetical statements in the same phrase or sentence so that a thing or a quality and its opposite are simultaneously brought to the reader's attention. The most noticeable use of this technique is whenever the question of Don Quixote's madness comes up. Then antithetical comments about his mental state, such as that he is a 'sane madman and wise fool', abound. But even when the matter referred to is of scant importance (and in the interpolated stories as well as in the story of the knight and his squire), the attraction for Cervantes of antithesis of this kind seems irresistible, as if he needed to avoid making unambiguous statements, or had a kind of compulsion to remind his readers how quite opposing qualities often coexist in the same person or situation. Thus we are told that one of the Toledan merchants Don Quixote meets on his first sally was 'a bit of a joker and very very prudent' (I.4). Describing his own appearance the knight remarks: 'I understand well, Sancho, that I am not good-looking but I also know that I am not deformed' (II.58). On another occasion, when a new humiliation has made him too upset to eat, he comments *à propos* of Sancho's greed: 'I, Sancho, was born to live dying and you to die eating' (II.59). Wishing to describe the drooping Rocinante unexpectedly responding to the advances of a nearby mare, Cervantes writes of the horse: 'being, after all, of flesh and blood, though he seemed as if he were of wood . . . ' (I.43). Such examples of antithesis exist by the hundred in the book. They echo stylistically the dualistic patterns of character and situation that run through it. In comic contexts such antitheses act as miniature units of comic incongruity whose effect is cumulative. Looked at more generally, Cervantes's addiction to antithetical utterance seems to point to some unconscious dichotomy of vision when he wrote this book.

Cervantes's success as a stylist owes much to the enormous linguistic range that he seems able so effortlessly to command. It reflects not only wide reading but also a life lived in many different kinds of milieu: thus soldier's talk, the koine used by Christian prisoners of the Turks, the special argot employed by criminals, and the specialized terminology of the gambling fraternity find a place in the prose of *Don Quixote* alongside reminiscences of the formalized language of notarial documents, phrases employed by ecclesiastical administrators and the kind of

Latin tags used, or misused, by educated show-offs. These and many other forms of special speech are brought into play, usually for comic effect but also simply because Cervantes is a lover of language and enjoys his ability to bend Spanish prose to his will. He does not shrink from inventing, when he needs it, a new word; since Don Quixote is sure that what is in fact an ordinary barber's basin is the helmet of a hero of romance—Mambrino— Cervantes coins a word for it that combines both views— *baciyelmo*, or 'basin-helmet'. Ridiculous, non-existent variations on conventional word forms are also occasionally invented. Sometimes, too, Cervantes, again to achieve a comic effect, will resort to extremely forced metaphorical comparisons. There is a good example of this in the decidedly unladylike language used by the false Dulcinea to address Sancho in Part II.35. Starting from the assertion by this Dulcinea (who is really an adolescent page-boy of the Duke) that grief at her enchanted condition makes tears drip continuously from her eyes ('in threads' as the Spanish idiom used has it), she then proceeds to upgrade the metaphor by restating it in the form of an assertion that she is weeping not threads but veritable skeins of tears. When she proceeds to describe the effect of so much weeping on her appearance she likens her cheeks to fields crossed by furrows, roads, and tracks. Language and style, then, confirm that Cervantes, when he wrote this book, was primarily concerned with creating a comic work on an epic scale.

So it was certainly interpreted by European readers for a long time. The idea that comic writing was by its very nature necessarily an inferior form to tragedy had not yet gained the acceptance it was to do nearer our own time. This was still a period when an authority of the status of Dr Samuel Johnson could assert that the greatness of Shakespeare's genius was more lastingly revealed in his comedies than in his tragedies. By the middle of the century, however, the occasional non-Spanish voice could be heard suggesting that *Don Quixote* was something more than a funny book. One of its English translators, Charles Jarvis, declared over-enigmatically (1742) that there were 'nicer beauties' in it than most readers supposed. But it was Johnson himself who first signalled unambiguously that new ways of interpreting the work were in the making. He made the good point that, although the knight was a ridiculous figure he was never a contemptible one and, writing in 1750, he even allowed pity as well as mirth to be a possible reader's response to him. It was Johnson, too, who declared that, when Cervantes described the fantasies of his hero, he was admitting to literature the species of imaginings (though usually of a different sort) which most readers, if they were honest, would admit privately to having. The inner imagination thus enters the world of realistic prose fiction disguised as madness. Johnson here gets near to inviting readers of *Don Quixote* to identify themselves with the mad knight on the grounds that this madness was no more than the workings of ordinary human imagination writ large. This represented a radical change in traditional attitudes to the book. It heralded the coming of its root-and-branch reappraisal by Romanticism. Whether Cervantes himself could have understood Johnson's interpretation of his book must, in the light of what we have seen in the present chapter, be rated unlikely.

8 Don Quixote as Romantic hero

The general theme [of *Don Quixote*] is the Real doing battle against the Ideal. (F. W. Schelling, *Philosophie der Kunst*, 1802–5)

Cervantes was too great a genius to make an extended joke out of a case of fortuitous madness and vulgar imbecility. (Jean Paul Richter, *Vorschule der Aesthetik*, 1804)

Some people have considered *Don Quixote* to be the saddest book that has ever been written; the moral teaching of the work, the fundamental idea behind it, is, indeed, deeply sad. (J. C. Simonde de Sismondi, *De la littérature du Midi de l'Europe*, III, 1814)

Samuel Johnson's readiness to admit that there was, perhaps, something more than amusement to be drawn from *Don Quixote* was not immediately followed up. In Spain and among European readers generally the traditional view continued to prevail until near the end of the eighteenth century. As late as 1798, a Spanish editor informed his readers unambiguously that the book was a burlesque which worked by ridiculing its hero. The Romantic reappraisal of the book was initiated in the opening years of the nineteenth century by some German Idealist philosophers concerned to work out the implications for art of their doctrines. Don Quixote was no longer seen just as a madman defending his absurd hallucinatory view of the world against everybody else's sane interpretation; he was now transformed primarily into a heroic defender of noble ideas in the face of all those who are ready to settle for the commonplace shallowness of things as they are. This does not mean that the sponsors of the new Romantic view attempted to deny the presence of the comic in Cervantes's book. They allowed the comedy to remain but treated it increasingly as time went on as merely a tool used by him to open up access to his real meaning. Jean Paul Richter thus asserted that Cervantes never allowed madness and laughter to appear unmixed with sanity and seriousness—an assertion which is only partly true and which, in any case, overlooks the fact that, in the mixture, the first two components preponderate.

Influential literary historians of the time soon went further, claiming that the real impression derived from reading *Don Quixote* was one of sadness, as in Sismondi's comment quoted above. Another influential German critic of the time, Friedrich Bouterwek, seized on the presence of the interpolated stories in the book as proof of 'how far Cervantes was from the idea attributed to him of writing a book merely to excite laughter' (1804). The new interpretation of the work passed into English poetry in the 1820s in Byron's much quoted lines:

> Of all tales 'tis the saddest—and more sad
> Because it makes us smile.
> (*Don Juan*, Canto 13).

If Romanticism increasingly turned Don Quixote himself into a tragic hero determinedly fighting for the cause of the nobler aspirations of man, it tended to esteem Sancho Panza much less than earlier readers had done for Sancho was now cast in the unattractive role of chief spokesman for materialistic commonsense and self-interest.

The obvious problems that the actual text of the book presented to anyone wishing to interpret it in these new ways were dealt with by various means. The knight's madness was the first matter that had to be disposed of. Here a solution was, of course, facilitated by the fact that one of the changes in social sensibility wrought by Romanticism was that madness was no longer thought to be a phenomenon at which it was permissible to laugh. Insanity was a tragic, pathetic malady but one, perhaps, also capable of insights denied to reason. However Cervantes's undoubted insistence that his mad knight was at least superficially comical limited the scope for interpreting his insanity along these lines, and Romantic critics preferred simply to play down the madness. Bouterwek thus described Don Quixote as 'the immortal representative of all men of exalted imagination who carry the noblest enthusiasm to the point of folly'. This notion that the knight's madness is no more than a manifestation of great imaginative powers carried too far has become a commonplace of Cervantine criticism. Imagination was often, also, equated with 'poetic imagination' and this, for the Romantics, provided another way out of the difficulty posed by the knight's madness; if he seemed to mistake reality, that was only because he interpreted it like a poet, in a symbolic or metaphorical way.

Cervantes's claim that he was concerned to kill off the taste for chivalric romance was also a difficulty, partly because it could not be accepted that a work of genius like this could be motivated by so trivial a purpose. But there was also the point that chivalric romance, with its concern for the heroic, and its use of the supernatural, its reliance on symbolism and its absolute determination to have no truck with everyday reality, enjoyed a renewal of popularity in the Romantic period. It became fashionable therefore to deny that Cervantes had any intention of attacking the romances at all or, alternatively, to assert that if he had started his novel with that intention, he soon abandoned it for more transcendental goals. Bouterwek hinted, in this connection, at a possibility that was to be seized on by some Spanish critics a century later: perhaps Cervantes himself was not fully aware of what was happening as he wrote his book. This idea was, however, at odds with another one also much favoured: *Don Quixote* was a kind of spiritual autobiography of its author; since he undoubtedly often alluded in it to objective events taken directly from his own personal experience, it was not unreasonable to suppose that, through the medium of appropriate symbols, he also gave literary shape to subjective aspects of that experience.

When they turned to the question of *Don Quixote* as a literary form, the Romantics found already to hand in it many of the qualities they thought the Romantic novel should have. It was, they claimed, poetic in tone and epic in structure and scope. Its hero was not confined to everyday human dimensions but expanded beyond these to achieve a symbolic stature that transcended the particular society and epoch in which he originated. The sheer inventiveness of Cervantes and the size of the canvas as he had painted it imitated the prodigality of Nature as the Romantic novelist must seek to do. That much vaunted Romantic quality, enthusiasm, was clearly there too, both in the ceaseless activity of Don Quixote himself and in the zestful creativity of the author. Predictably, Dulcinea del Toboso now became a key figure for understanding the book's purpose. The element of burlesque that Cervantes had seemed always careful to surround her with has gone and she has become the chief symbol of the Ideal for which Don Quixote fights. She is now presented as the authentic grand passion of the knight's life and also as the eternal personification of unattainable 'Absolute Love'.

One important achievement of Romanticism was that it not only entirely changed the language of *Quixote* criticism; its new interpretation of the book enormously increased the range of possible critical discussion by releasing the critic from the constraints that face him when he attempts to discuss the comic. From the Ancient World to modern times writers have complained of these difficulties. One is the obvious fact that one cannot discuss humour in humorous terms, only in serious ones. Another stems from the nature of the comic itself. Even the subtlest forms of comedy (satire, various forms of word-play, irony), appeal to the intellect, not to the emotions. Other forms (parody, burlesque, or farce, for example) are quite incompatible with the serious emotions; dignity, fear, or pity cannot coexist with laughter. The callousness that the comic requires is, as we have seen, a notable aspect of the way Cervantes treats Don Quixote and Sancho Panza. A further problem for the critic lies in the fact that laughter is a mechanistic, physical response to a situation; it does not lend itself to analysis or sustained scrutiny any more than do the feelings it may leave behind it—pleasure, merriment, even happiness. A joke explained is a joke killed. Whatever we may think of Romanticism's determination to view Cervantes's tale as one in which tragedy predominated over comedy and one with which the reader was now invited to identify himself, it cannot be denied that it made criticism free to deploy new emotive responses to the book in wide-ranging speculations often couched in affective imagery and metaphor. This is to be seen, for example, in the pages that Victor Hugo devotes to Cervantes's book in his essay on William Shakespeare. When Hugo, who paid more attention to the comic aspects of *Don Quixote* than did most Romantics, described Cervantes as a Homeric buffoon like Rabelais, he made an assertion which, although it can hardly survive analysis, nevertheless sticks in the mind. Even Hugo, though, did not allow comedy to be Cervantes's principal purpose. One might, he wrote, suspect the Spanish author of having attempted to mock ideals, but that was a defect more apparent than real. If one looked carefully it would be seen that the smile was accompanied by a tear and that, in reality, Cervantes is on Don Quixote's side. Hugo's likening of Don Quixote mounted on Rocinante to 'heroism mounted on fatigue' is another of his memorable metaphors.

How was such a sea-change in the interpretation of the

book possible? First it should be noted that most of the critics whose works have been referred to (and the many others who followed the same lines) depended on rather indifferent translations into their own language or were insufficiently equipped in Spanish to pick up or to appreciate fully the ceaseless verbal comedy in which Cervantes indulges. Cervantes's reliance on verbal antithesis and on paradox often made the new interpretation appear to work, when managed selectively so that attention was concentrated on that part of the antithesis or paradox that served the critic's purpose. But the main reason for the enthusiasm which *Don Quixote* aroused in the Romantics was that it seemed to provide figures ready-made to serve the purposes of Romantic mythology. The German theorists of Romanticism had noted the need to find new mythic figures to act as symbols of the situation of modern man in a manner comparable to the ways in which ancient myths had served in antiquity. Don Quixote and Sancho Panza, in particular, once their comic context had been pushed into the background, seemed specially created to symbolize the struggle between idealism and bourgeois materialism that was central to much Romantic thinking. Since myth is, by definition, not subject to any sanction of proof, it then really ceased to matter if Cervantes had intended his characters to have any such metaphorical function or, even, whether the totality of his text allowed it.

The radical reinterpretation of *Don Quixote* carried out in the early years of the nineteenth century is not simply a past chapter in the continuing story of readers' responses to the book. The Romantic approach, or attitudes derived directly from it have continued to dominate much criticism down to the present time. These attitudes have also affected those of modern translators of the book from Spanish, so making the Romantic approach spuriously self-fulfilling. One example illustrates the point. In Part I.19 Don Quixote has his face smashed and his teeth knocked out by stones thrown at him by some shepherds whom he has annoyed. Sancho thereupon attaches to his name the new descriptive epithet 'Caballero de la Triste Figura' which Thomas Shelton, in 1612, correctly translated from the Spanish as 'Knight of the Ill-Favoured Face'—a comment on the knight's smashed-up visage. Modern translators however regularly come up with linguistically anachronistic phrases like 'Knight of the Sad Countenance' or 'Sir Knight of the Sorrowful Figure', with their deliberate implications of superior, even Christlike, suffering. Were we dealing with a modern Spanish writer, such a translation would be permissible; used here, it simply fails to translate Cervantes's ironic words or convey the situation he has taken pains to explain.

Quixote criticism has, since the middle of the nineteenth century, usually adopted the Romantic position with enthusiasm, often to the extent that no mention is even made by the critic of the knight's madness or the comic aspects of the book. The symbolic interpretation favoured by the Romantics has proved a particularly durable influence on the critics. One of them, the twentieth-century philosopher Ortega y Gasset, used the symbolism he detected in the book to illustrate the artistic consequences of his philosophy. He frankly admitted, though, that it was hard to document his interpretation from the text itself. He wrote:

> No other book exists whose capacity for alluding, through symbols, to the universal meaning of life is so great; yet there is no other book, either, in which we find fewer hints and fewer signals concerning the way it is to be interpreted.

In fact, as we have seen, Cervantes's book is, of course, full of signals to the reader about how to interpret it. What it does not offer are any hints to support the kind of interpretation which Ortega wishes to find there. Miguel de

Unamuno, writing at the beginning of this century, was less bothered by Ortega's point. It did not matter in the slightest to his interpretation, he said, either what Cervantes's intention was or what he had actually put in his book: 'What lives', Unamuno wrote, 'is what I find there, whether Cervantes put it there or not.' It is hard sometimes not to feel that Unamuno said out loud what many critics put into practice in silence, as, for instance, when we read that Cervantes reveals himself in *Don Quixote* and his other works as a secret follower of the unorthodoxies of Erasmus, forced to conceal his radicalism beneath a veil of religious hypocrisy, or that he was a secret New Christian (the name given to Spanish Christians of Jewish ancestry) whose work expresses in disguised fashion the discontents and resentments of that racial minority. Marxist interpretations of *Don Quixote* see the book as a study in alienation and as the product of a society in which the conflict is between the desire to be one kind of person and the dying social institutions and distorted economic forces that compel one to live as someone else. It should be noted, however, that Marx himself, who had a special admiration for *Don Quixote*, speaks of it in the terms made familiar by the German Romantics.

As a Romantic hero Don Quixote, with Sancho Panza, has passed irrevocably into opera, ballet, films, and the theatre as well as into the metaphorical commonplaces of many languages. The book, interpreted in the Romantic tradition, has inspired many distinguished writers and critics. This approach is, then, now a permanent part of the history of the literary and other arts. It is nevertheless true that, while we may find the Romantic Don Quixote as a shadowy personage lurking at times in the pages of the book that bears his name, those characters who are plainly and continuously present are the mad knight, his *alter ego*, the foolish but astute squire, and all the other comically-contexted figures whom Cervantes has told us to expect. It is a curious paradox of Romantic criticism that, by turning away from the text Cervantes actually wrote towards the myth which has achieved a separate existence from the book, it seems to turn its back on the reality before its eyes in exactly the determined way the knight himself did. This is why much of today's critical writing about *Don Quixote* in the Romantic tradition often leaves its readers, when they turn from the critic to Cervantes's book itself, with the baffled feeling that they have been led to expect something that is not there. On the other hand, when the book is read as Cervantes directs us to read it, everything falls naturally into place and the whole work reads as a coherent, if loosely knit, entity in which language, style, plot, situations, and characters are all directed towards a comic purpose. If, from time to time, something that is said, or something that happens, seems to introduce an ambiguous suggestion of melancholy, or a reaching out towards the hidden seriousness that usually adheres to laughter, that only enhances and deepens the comedy. It does not turn comedy into tragedy. Since comic writing that has the quality of genius is even rarer than great tragedy it seems a pity gratuitously to reject *Don Quixote* in the form Cervantes offers it to us. As for the knight as Romantic hero, it is, of course, doubtful, because he was mad, if we can properly call Don Quixote a hero at all. Strictly speaking, his heroics depend on a misreading of the odds akin to that of the drug addict who jumps from a high window believing that he can fly.

9 Conclusion

Don Quixote in no way represented a rejection by Cervantes of the romance form in general. The attractions and potential merits of the genre had been defended by the canon of Toledo in Part I. 48—a defence all the more explicable if, as has been suggested, Cervantes had already by then begun work on *The Labours of Persiles and Sigismunda*. The *Persiles*, posthumously published in 1617, was, by his own admission, Cervantes's bid to show his peers that, as well as being a master of comic prose fiction, he could, in serious vein, even surpass the achievement of Heliodorus, whose *Ethiopian History*, written some fourteen hundred years earlier, was regarded by Renaissance scholars as the model of what romance ought to be. Faithful to the dualistic attitude so frequently to be found in his writing, Cervantes, while writing his parody of chivalric romance, had concurrently been working on his attempt to compete with Heliodorus.

Cervantes subtitled his new work 'a northern story' because the action of the first two of its four books takes place partly in the frozen Arctic and in Scandinavia, regions that Cervantes only knew about from books but whose remoteness, he believed, would permit him to locate extraordinary events there without straining the credulity of his Spanish readers too much.

In accordance with the formal traditions of epic poetry as followed by Heliodorus's prose, the new work's narrative begins in the middle of things, working from there both forwards and backwards. Basically it is the story of a pilgrimage to Rome from the barbarian northern fringes of Europe made by a royal prince and princess, Persiles and Sigismunda, who are secret but chaste lovers, until their arrival in Rome after overcoming many obstacles clears the way for them to marry and return home to rule their two kingdoms. In keeping with Cervantes's reliance in this book on disguise and mystery of every sort, neither the reader nor anyone else except the royal couple is supposed to know until near the end that they are Persiles and Sigismunda; they pass themselves off as brother and sister called Periandro and Auristela.

The contrast between this book and *Don Quixote* is startling. A description of its basic plot can give no idea of its narrative complexities as Cervantes's inventiveness releases a flood of story-telling. The interlacing narrative technique that always attracted him is here used to set up intricate cat's cradles that sometimes even the author is hard put to it to unmesh. Cruel barbarians, fierce pirates and bandits, kidnappings, threats of rape, murder and human sacrifice, ships crewed by vengeful women, monstrous animals, mysterious natural phenomena, shipwrecks, as well as a plethora of more commonplace vicissitudes, play their part in setting up the ordeals which the characters must face to establish their heroic stature. Cervantes introduces many characters simply so that they can tell their own particular story. At all times, in the conversational as well as the descriptive passages, the prose maintains a high tone befitting the epic style and unremitting moral purpose of this kind of romance. For good measure the intention of the narrative is often overtly allegorical. In the last two books, where the action moves to more familiar lands, Cervantes allows the epic mode to be incongruously invaded at times by material drawn from everyday reality. Thus there are unexpected commentaries on the contemporary social and artistic scene in Spain, including yet another criticism of the drama cultivated by Lope de Vega. Occasionally Cervantes now even reverts to the comic and satirical mode of *Don Quixote* with a zest which makes the reader wonder just how far his heart by now really was in the huge creative task his imitation of

Heliodorus had committed him to. The Prologue to this work, written on his deathbed, is unexpectedly if ironically jocose and insists explicitly on his reputation as a comic writer. It says nothing about the book he is supposed to be introducing. One may legitimately ask if Cervantes had not perhaps at the end finally come to recognize that it was as a comic genius that he had been destined to excel.

Persiles and Sigismunda is, on its own terms, a creative *tour de force*, specially when we remember the age of the man who wrote it. The non-specialist reader today will probably only find to his taste in the early parts of the story some of the fine descriptive passages it contains. Thus the description of the shipwreck at the beginning of Book II, though written in the mannered style Cervantes favours in this work, is among the most effective pieces of Spanish Golden Age descriptive prose. Cervantes, it should be remembered, was one of the very few writers of prose fiction of his time to specialize in maritime scenes. His determination to appeal to a scholarly readership is responsible for the displays of erudition and sententious comment that characterize the book, though it cannot be claimed that Cervantes, here more than anywhere else, contributes anything original to the general history of ideas. The work had a certain amount of success when it was first published, showing that Cervantes had correctly assessed the literary taste of some readers of the time. It continued to find a limited readership as long as a taste for romance in the late-Greek tradition lasted. But, for most European readers of prose fiction since the seventeenth century, Cervantes's name is associated only with his authorship of *Don Quixote*, though, specially in Spain and France, his *Exemplary Novels* have also enjoyed considerable repute.

As we saw at the beginning of this study, critics from many lands have seen in *Don Quixote* the harbinger and sometimes the prototype of the modern novel. An impressive array of novelists themselves have expressed similar opinions. It is easy to see why eighteenth-century novelists like Fielding or Lesage did so, because they cultivated the burlesque epic style Cervantes had used. The connection between Cervantes's book and the forms taken by the novel in later times is, however, more elusive. A parodic or even a more generally comic stance is hardly the norm in the modern novel. Cervantes's attitude to contemporary reality in the book is certainly not that favoured by the great nineteenth-century realists. The daily scene appears in *Don Quixote* not because the author thinks it interesting or important in its own right; we have to turn to some of the *Exemplary Novels* for examples of that. In *Don Quixote* everyday reality is only brought to our notice in so far as the confrontational parody requires its presence. As the French novelist Gustave Flaubert, himself a great reader of Cervantes's book, noted, the high roads of Spain on which so much of the action takes place are never described. The same can be said of the roadside inns which figure so largely in the book; we can infer a great deal about them from what happens there but they do not ever earn any description for description's sake. In Part II, though many chapters take place in the ducal palace, the reader would be hard put to it either to describe the palace, or what routine life there was like when neither Don Quixote nor Sancho was visiting. Nor does the book anticipate the assumption of later novelists that to understand a character's present we must know a good deal about his past. Cervantes resolutely refuses to tell us anything much about Don Quixote's life before middle age and madness came upon him and he treats the past of his other characters in the same way. This attitude must be deliberate. A long tradition of realistic fiction had existed in Spain since the end of the fifteenth century; Cervantes himself engaged in it in some of his other works. If he does not do so in *Don Quixote* it is presumably because, there, he is only concerned with catching his characters and their situations when they are highlighted by comedy. In those circumstances background description would have been not only an irrelevant but a positively counterproductive piece of authorial self-indulgence.

The ambiguity of the book is another feature that we scarcely associate with the modern novel. Novelists have usually sought to persuade their readers that the fictional tale they are looking at seems as if it were historically true even if they know it is not. Cervantes, anticipating experiments with the novel in our own time, deliberately sets out to warn his readers not to put too much trust in the authenticity of the text he offers them, or even in the authority of its various authors. Curiously enough the result of such frankness is to increase, not diminish, the conviction the book carries.

Ambiguity, which is built in to the book's formal structure as well as into its treatment of plot, characters, and theme, continues even after, at the end of Part II, Don Quixote recovers his sanity. We expect him then, in his recuperated personality as Alonso Quijano, to recognize that Don Quixote was a mere hallucinatory figment of his imagination. The dying man, however, merely says that he *was* Don Quixote and has become again Alonso Quijano. The final paradox is that Don Quixote cannot ever be displaced by his sane self. He is the chief figure of a book bearing his name and will continue to exist as long as men and women read novels. It is his 'real' self, Alonso Quijano, who is doomed to death followed by obscurity. It is hard not to believe that, when he wrote this scene, the ailing Cervantes was not aware of the affinity between the ex-knight's situation and his own but we, of course, get no overt suggestion of this.

Any discussion of the influence of *Don Quixote* on the modern novel needs to start by accepting the premiss enunciated by the critic Georg Lukács when he wrote of Cervantes's book that, like most great novels, it 'had to remain the only important objectivation of its type'. There have been a number of imitations of *Don Quixote*—the best of them being that of Avellaneda—but the imitations only serve to underline the uniqueness of Cervantes's genius. Yet, despite the differences just referred to, it is not difficult to see why novelists and critics alike have stressed the book's progenitive role in the history of the novel. There were other Spanish books, all widely read and admired throughout sixteenth-century Europe, which seem, more than *Don Quixote* does, to anticipate the rise of the realistic novel of later times—works like the famous *Tragicomedy of Calisto and Melibea* (better known as *La Celestina*) or picaresque novels like *Lazarillo de Tormes* or *Guzmán de Alfarache*. But these do not have the mythical significance that gives to Cervantes's book its enigmatic and timeless appeal or the extra dimension it owes to the fact that, though parodying chivalric romance, like Ariosto before him, its author's mockery of the chivalry books is mingled with understanding of and respect for the ideas that they sought to express. There is a parallel here with the way in which the insane Don Quixote and the foolish Sancho, however laughable their ridiculous antics and utterances may be, are never quite stripped by Cervantes of his dignity in the case of the knight or his self-respect in the case of the squire. Thanks, too, to the fact that the book is written in the comic mode, which freed it from any obligation to bow to contemporary notions of literary (or social) decorum, Cervantes was able to show the potentially unrestricted scope of narrative registers at a novelist's disposal.

There are a number of other likenesses between *Don Quixote* and the modern novel. The book's underlying theme, the confrontation of illusion with reality, prefigures in its own special way a topic that has been a staple of later novelists. Cervantes's view in it that irony provides the most appropriate stance for a novelist to adopt in order to report on the human condition has also often proved a fruitful one in the subsequent history of the novel, as has his penchant, in this case not peculiar to *Don Quixote*, for showing the multiple perspectives which result when different characters view the same thing. Also important, specially for writers themselves, is the fact that, by his insistence on asking questions about the nature of fiction and about its difficult relationship to truth and to the reality it purports to portray and analyse, Cervantes made it obligatory for all subsequent novelists who take themselves seriously to think about the nature of the enterprise on which they are engaged. Nor should the liberating laughter that echoes through the greater part of *Don Quixote*, often at the expense of romance and other forms of literature, be allowed to obscure the fact that the book is an assertion of the power of literature as an art form. This is not only because, in the person of the knight, Cervantes shows us literature taking entire control of a life and through him greatly affecting the daily lives of many others; it is also because in it he demonstrated that, to be a writer of originality and genius, one did not have to hold new or interesting general beliefs or purvey some clear-cut intellectual message. What matters in *Don Quixote* is the artistic vision and its author's mastery of the techniques he needed to bring that vision to full fruition. In an age when, in Counter-Reformation Spain, dogma and certainty supposedly ruled, Cervantes demonstrated in his most famous book how ambiguity and uncertainty could lie at the centre of great art. He was only able to do so by showing that great art could be comic art.

Further reading

These suggestions confine themselves to books and articles in English except when the only satisfactory treatment of a topic is in Spanish or French.

1. Bibliography

Useful for English-speaking readers is Dana B. Drake, *Don Quijote (1894–1970): A Selective Annotated Bibliography*, I (Chapel Hill, N. C., 1974); II (Miami, Florida, 1978); III (New York, 1980). Up-to-date Cervantes bibliography (in Spanish) is maintained in *Anales cervantinos*, I–IX (1951–62); X– (1971–).

For readers able to read the Spanish text the best modern edition of *Don Quixote* is the helpfully annotated one of L. A. Murillo, 2 vols (Castalia: Madrid, 1973).

2. Translations

DON QUIXOTE:

The most accessible translation of *Don Quixote* is that by J. M. Cohen (Penguin Books, 1950; repr. 1968). This is a straightforward modernizing version; it is over-inclined to take the easy way out when faced with the difficulties Cervantes's ways of using language present to any translator. The best modern translation as far as fidelity to the original text is concerned is still that of John Ormsby (London, 1885). There is a modern edition of Thomas Shelton's translation (1612, 1620) in the Tudor Translations series, vols XIII–XVI (London, 1896; repr. New York, 1967). For a comparative study of the worth of various English translations of *Don*

Quixote see S. A. Gerhard, *Don Quixote and the Shelton Translation* (Madrid, 1982).

OTHER WORKS:

Galatea (in *The Complete Works*, ed. J. Fitzmaurice-Kelly, Glasgow, 1901–3).

Exemplarie Novells in Sixe Books, trans. by James Mabbe (London, 1640; repr. London and Philadelphia, 1900). Mabbe translated only those tales that modern critics often label 'idealistic' or 'romantic'; six of those more closely concerned with depicting or satirizing aspects of Spanish society in Cervantes's time will be found in the translation of C. A. Jones, *Exemplary Stories* (Penguin Books, 1972).

Journey to Parnassus, bilingual trans. by J. V. Gibson (London, 1883).

Interludes [*Entremeses*], trans. by Edwin Honig (New York, 1964).

3. General

Bardon, M., *Don Quichotte en France au XVIIᵉ et au XVIIIᵉ siècle: 1605–1815*, 2 vols (Paris, 1931); Castro, Américo, *El pensamiento de Cervantes* (1st. edn, Madrid 1925, —preferable to 2nd edn, Barcelona, 1972); El Saffar, Ruth, *Distance and Control in 'Don Quixote': A Study in Narrative Technique* (Chapel Hill, N. C., 1975); Entwistle, William J., *Cervantes* (Oxford, 1940; repr. 1965, 1967); Forcione, Alban K., *Cervantes, Aristotle and the 'Persiles'* (Princeton, N. J., 1970); Hazard, Paul, *Don Quichotte de Cervantès. Étude et analyse* (Paris, 1931; repr. 1949); Levin, Harry, 'The Example of Cervantes', in *Contexts of Criticism* (New York, 1963); Madariaga, Salvador de, *Don Quixote: An Introductory Essay in Psychology* (Oxford, 1935); Nelson Jr., L. (ed.), *Cervantes: A Collection of Critical Essays* (Englewood Cliffs, N. J., 1969) —a number of essays on Cervantes by Auden, Levin, Brenan, Thomas Mann, and other critics and writers; Riley, E. C., *Cervantes's Theory of the Novel* (Oxford, 1962); Torrente Ballester, Gonzalo, *El 'Quijote' como juego*. [The 'Quixote' as a Game] (Madrid, 1975).

Further reading

The following recent general studies of the European and American novel may be found helpful by readers wishing to examine the relationship of *Don Quixote* to the modern novel in greater depth:

Allott, Miriam, *Novelists on the Novel* (London, 1959); Booth, Wayne C., *The Rhetoric of Fiction* (2nd edn, Chicago and London, 1983); D. C. Muecke, *The Compass of Irony* (London and New York, 1969; repr. 1980); Ian Watt, *The Rise of the Novel* (London, 1957; repr. Penguin Books, 1983).

Chapters 1 and 2: Byron, W., *Cervantes: A Biography* (New York, 1978); McKendrick, Mulveena, *Cervantes* (Boston, Mass., 1980).

Chapter 3. Williamson, Edwin, *The Half-Way House of Fiction. Don Quixote and Arthurian Romance* (Oxford, 1984); Eisenberg, Daniel, 'Don Quijote and the Romances of Chivalry: the need for a reexamination', *Hispanic Review*, 41, 1953.

Chapters 4 and 5: Willis, Jr., Raymond S., *The Phantom Chapters of the 'Quijote'* (New York, 1953); Williamson, Edwin, 'Romance and Realism in the Interpolated Stories of the *Quixote'*, *Cervantes*, 2, 1982.

Chapter 6: Bigeard, Martine, *La Folie et les fous littéraires en Espagne* (Paris, 1972); Samuel Butler, *Characters and Passages from Note-Books*, ed. A. R. Waller (Cambridge, 1908), *passim*.

Chapter 7: Auerbach, Erich, 'The Enchanted Dulcinea' in *Mimesis. The Representation of Reality in Western Literature* (New York, 1953); Bergson, Henri, *Laughter. An Essay on the Meaning of the Comic*, trans. C. Brereton and F. Rothwell (London, 1913); Close, Anthony, 'Sancho Panza: Wise Fool', *Modern Language Review*, 68, 1973; Rosenblat, Ángel, *La lengua del 'Quijote'* (Madrid, 1971; repr. 1978); Russell, P. E., 'Don Quixote as a Funny Book', *Modern Language Review*, 64, 1969.

Chapter 8: Close, Anthony, *The Romantic Approach to 'Don Quixote'* (Cambridge, 1978).

Chapter 9: For Heliodorus and the late Greek romance in

general see Elizabeth Haight, *Essays on the Greek Romances* (New York, 1943). For a modern study of *The Labours of Persiles and Sigismunda* see the relevant chapters of Forcione, Alban K., *Cervantes, Aristotle and the Persiles* (Princeton, N. J., 1970). An accessible modern translation of Heliodorus's romance is that of Sir W. Lamb, *Ethiopian Story* (London and New York, 1961).

Index

Amadis of Gaul, 26–7, 39, 51
Ariosto, Ludovico, 10, 16, 27, 62, 108
'Avellaneda', *see* 'Fernández de Avellaneda, Alonso'

Barataria, island of, 66
Barcelona, 67–71
Bouterwek, Friedrich, 95–6
Butler, Samuel, 74
Byron, Lord, 95

Calisto and Melibea, Tragicomedy of, 108
'Camacho's Wedding', 61
canon of Toledo, 28–9
'Captive Captain, The', 11
'Cardenio and Dorotea', 49
Carrasco, Sansón, 56–7, 59, 71, 76–7
CERVANTES, Saavedra, Miguel de:
  birth, 6
  education, 7–9
  enlists in army, 6, 9–10
  captivity in Algiers, 10–11
  authorship, early attempts at, 13–17, 23
  marriage, 18, 22
  commissary of the Armada in Andalusia, 18–20
  imprisoned, 19
  last years, 20–2
  death of, 22–3
  PUBLICATIONS:
  La Galatea, 5, 12, 14–17
  Don Quixote, Part I, 5, 20–1, 64, 70, and *passim*

Exemplary Novels, 5, 9, 19
A Voyage to Parnassus, 5, 21
Don Quixote, Part II, 5, 55, 72, and *passim*
Eight Comedies and Eight Interludes, 6
The Labours of Persiles and Sigismunda, 6, 18, 22, 103
CERVANTES and:
  criminal classes, the, 20, 68
  family life, 6–7, 20–1
  Islam, 11
  military life, 3, 12
  pastoral romance, 14–17
  poetry, 13, 16–18, 60
  romances of chivalry, 24–37
  theatre, the, 9, 13–14
Cide Hamete Benengeli, 52–3
'Colloquy of the Dogs, The', 7

Defoe, Daniel, 86
Diana, La, 15
DON QUIXOTE:
  English translations of, 2
  French translations of, 2–3
  printed in England, 3
  seventeenth-century interpretations of, 85–6
  eighteenth-century interpretations of, 93–4
  Romantic interpretations of, 49, 80–1, 94–102
  modern interpretations of, 99–101
  TOPICS TREATED IN:
  appearance and reality, 42, 47–8, 61–3, 87
  arms and letters, 51

115

Index

author's intention, 24–5, 40, 88, 96

balladry, 26, 61–4

chivalric romance, 24, 28–9, 51–2, 71, 73–4, 96, 108

Golden Age, 50

STYLE AND TECHNIQUE IN:

ambiguity, 26–7, 39, 40–1, 75–6, 107, 109

antithesis, 90–1

authors, multiplicity of suggested, 3, 32, 52–3

comic purpose, 25, 40, 44, 51, 54, 63, 64, 73, 81, 82–93, 95, 100, 102, 109

farce, 41, 43, 83

fiction, its nature probed, 53, 57, 65, 67–8, 109

interpolated stories, role of, 48–9, 95

irony, examples of, 54, 60, 80, 84

language, Cervantes's use of, 87–92

laughter aroused, 40, 52, 82–4, 86–7, 95, 98, 109

narrative structure, 4, 17, 36–9

novel, modern, *DQ* as paradigm of, 1, 105–9

parody, 24, 33–7, 62, 73, 83, 85 and *passim*

Part I and Part II, differences between, 55–6, 72

stylistic characteristics, 75, 83, 88–92, 99

symbolic interpretation, 97, 100

DON QUIXOTE (as character):

'Avellaneda', response to, 21–2, 66–8

death of, 71

'enchanters', role of, 53–4, 58–9, 63, 76

fame, desire for, 56

friends, treatment by, 83

home life of, 40–1

inauthenticity of, as knight, 34–5

library of, 17, 26

madness of, examined, 6, 34, 47–8, 60–1, 71, 73–8, 80–1, 84–5, 90–1, 93, 95–6, 100

moral responsibility, absence of, 77

name, origins of, 41

Part I: unread by him, 56–7

physical appearance of, 40, 74

programmed by romances, 34, 70, 76, 109

Sancho Panza, relationship with, 44–5, 72

Duke and Duchess introduced, 64–6; criticized, 77

Dulcinea del Toboso, 42, 46, 48, 57–8, 63, 65–7, 84, 92, 97

Erasmus, Desiderius, 8, 101

Esquivias, 18

Exemplary Novels, 9, 68, 105–6

'Fernández de Avellaneda, Alonso', 66–8, 70–1, 77

Fielding, Henry, 85, 106

Flaubert, Gustave, 106

'Glass Licenciate, The', 76

Guinart, Roque, 68

Guzmán de Alfarache, 108

Hassan Pasha, 11

Heliodorus, 103, 105

Hugo, Victor, 98

Jarvis, Charles, 93

Jesuits, 7–8

Johnson, Samuel, 92–4

Lazarillo de Tormes, 108

Lemos, Count of, 21
Lepanto, battle of, 9
Lesage, Alain-René, 106
Levin, Harry, 1
López Pinciano, Alonso, 86
Lorenzo, Aldonza, *see* Dulcinea del Toboso
Lukács, Georg, 107

Marx, Karl, 101
Miranda, Don Diego de, 60
Montemayor, Jorge de, 15
Moreno, Don Antonio, 68–9, 71, 76
mythification of Don Quixote, 2, 41, 99, 101–2, 108

Orlando Furioso (*see also* Ariosto), 10, 16, 22, 27–8, 62
Ortega y Gasset, José, 100
Oudin, César, 2–3

Panza, Sancho, 35, 44–5, 55–6, 58–9, 63–6, 71, 74–5, 78–80, 95
Panza, Teresa, 57, 79
parody, 10, 29, 33–4, 36–7, 52–3, 63
pastoral romance, characteristics of, 14–16
Persiles and Sigismunda, 6, 12, 18, 21–3, 69–70, 103–5

Quijano, Alonso (alias Don Quixote), 71, 107

Rapin, Père, 85
Reeve, Clara, 4
Richter, Jean Paul, 94–5
'Ricote, the Moor', story of, 69
Rocinante, 40
romance, defined, 4, 85
romances of chivalry, 9–10, 24–37, 64
Rosset, François de, 3

Saint-Évremond, Charles-Denis, sieur de, 87
Sancho Panza, *see* Panza, Sancho
Sandoval y Rojas, Bernado de, Archbishop of Toledo, 21
Sannazaro, Jacopo, 15
Saragossa, 54, 57, 66–8
Schelling, F. W., 94
Sergas de Esplandián, 51
Simonde de Sismondi, J. C., 94
Smollett, Tobias, 85
Steele, Richard, 85–6

Tarfe, Don Alvaro, 68

Unamuno, Miguel de, 100–1

Vega, Lope de, 14, 21, 104